THE CHURCH INSIDE OUT

PUBLISHER'S NOTE

Adventures in Faith is a series of books for people with inquiring minds. These writings represent the viewpoints of authors from differing traditions and various parts of the world. Some may offer frankly unorthodox interpretations of the Christian faith, while others may apply or adapt to new situations classic positions of the church. These books may either complement or contradict one another, but they share a common purpose to say something pertinent at the frontiers where the church meets the world today and where faith reaches out to meet the needs of the future.

THE CHURCH INSIDE OUT

by
J. C. Hoekendijk

Edited by
L. A. Hoedemaker and Pieter Tijmes

Translated by
Isaac C. Rottenberg

THE WESTMINSTER PRESS
Philadelphia

This book originally appeared as *De Kerk Bin-nenste Buiten*, W. Ten Have N. V., Amsterdam, 1964.

LIBRARY OF CONGRESS CATALOG CARD NO. 66–10600

Published by The Westminster Press ®
Philadelphia, Pennsylvania

PRINTED IN THE UNITED STATES OF AMERICA

TRANSLATOR'S NOTE

IN RECENT YEARS an increasing number of Dutch theologians have been introduced to the English-speaking world, either through translations or through discussion of their thought in articles and books written by those who are proficient in the Dutch language. From my own endeavors in this direction, I have gained the impression that there are quite a few people in the Anglo-Saxon world who welcome this opportunity to become thus better acquainted with theological developments in the Netherlands. I have therefore undertaken the task of translating these selections from the work of J. C. Hoekendijk in the hope that they would further contribute to an open and critical exchange in the world church on the questions that concern us all.

Dr. Hoekendijk's special interest in the themes of the mission of the church, ecumenics, parish renewal, and the lay movement remind one of the works of another Dutchman: Hendrik Kraemer. However, Hoekendijk is definitely a thinker in his own right, often quite original and quite controversial. This "troubler of Israel" deserves a hearing in the church today. Even those who do not agree with his answers will most probably be stimulated to deeper reflection on the questions he raises.

Dr. Hoekendijk is not altogether a stranger to many readers in the English-speaking world. Many of his articles have appeared in periodicals published on different continents and in different languages, including English. Thus, some of the chapters in this book are not my translations from the Dutch collection but are articles from English-language journals that have given permission for these materials to be republished here. Included are the following: Chapter I, "The Call to Evangelism," *International Review of Missions,* April, 1950; Chapter IX, "Safety Last" (original title: "Exceptions, Eschatology and Our Common Practices"), *Youth,* No. 6, December, 1962; Chapter X, "On the Way to the World of Tomorrow," *Laity,* No. 11, August, 1961. Also fragments, identified by numbers from the bibliography, are excerpted from "The Church in Missionary Thinking," *International Review of Missions,* July, 1952; and "Christ and the World in the Modern Age," *The Student World,* No. 1–2, 1961.

At Professor Hoekendijk's suggestion, Chapter IV, "A Changed Church in a Changed Society," was inserted to replace the selections that composed that chapter in the Dutch work. This was done because it was felt that some of the issues raised there are not as relevant to the American situation as they are to the European scene. Professor Hoekendijk has examined the manuscript for this English edition. L. A. Hoedemaker, one of the original editors of this collection, has reviewed the English version and has revised the editors' Foreword. He also has made suggestions concerning the translation of certain passages; but he is not responsible, of course, for the English text as it is here published.

I. C. R.

FOREWORD

IN THIS BOOK we have attempted to let Prof. J. C. Hoekendijk speak fully for himself by putting together several
parts of his work through the period from 1948 to 1964.
For the first time all the themes dealt with during those
years have been put into a conveniently arranged order.
Until now, Hoekendijk was known to the larger public only
through a few sensational articles. This unfortunate limi-
tation is no longer necessary, since we had access to all
publications, including many manuscripts.

The book is divided into two parts. In the first part,
"The Church as Function of the Apostolate" (Chapters
I to V), the material has been arranged systematically. It
includes complete articles (the first and fourth chapters
and the second part of the fifth chapter) and a series of
excerpts. In the second part, "The Encounter of Church
and World" (Chapters VI to X), we have gathered five
complete essays more or less as illustrations of the first
part. In the article on "Church and Race" a fragment
from elsewhere was included.

We have also added a bibliography, which is as complete as possible up to August, 1964. Each item of the
bibliography is numbered and these numbers are used in
the text at the end of a cited excerpt to identify the source
of the excerpt. For example, (32, 153–154) means: number 32 in the bibliography, pp. 153–154.

In connection with these references it is advisable to notice the year and the context of the relevant publications. Only at certain points have we taken small liberties, e.g., when the language of speech had to be put into writing style, or where the combining of excerpts necessitated small revisions. We have abbreviated the piece on the house church, since it was written in a specific context that is not wholly relevant here.

The title of the book, as well as the headings of the chapters, are ours, except in the case of Chapters I, VI, IX, and X.

Finally, we express our gratitude to Professor Hoekendijk for the assistance he has rendered and for his critical evaluation of the manuscript.

THE EDITORS

CONTENTS

I

THE CALL TO EVANGELISM

IT IS IMPOSSIBLE to ignore the call to evangelism, for it is
being raised in so many quarters of the world. The Amsterdam Assembly expressed the conviction of the churches
in these words:

> As we have studied evangelism in its ecumenical setting,
> we have been burdened by a sense of urgency. We have
> recaptured something of the spirit of the apostolic age,
> when the believers went everywhere preaching the Word.
> If the gospel really is a matter of life and death, it seems
> intolerable that any human being now in the world should
> live out his life, without ever having had the chance to
> hear and receive it. . . . Now, not tomorrow, is the time
> to act.

This sense of urgency is echoed to an ever-growing extent. Recently, forty denominations in the United States
launched a united evangelistic campaign. In the official
statement we read:

> The time is urgent. The call to advance rests upon the
> seriousness of the day in which we live; upon the authority
> of Christ; and upon the necessity of new life for all men
> through obedience and faith in Him.

A similar call to advance is voiced in other parts of the
world. Churches in Australia and Japan, in Hungary and
Germany, in Great Britain and Canada, prepare a new

and courageous evangelistic outreach into the areas lost to the church. And, meanwhile, the sober and less conspicuous evangelization in younger church areas is continued, without the clarion calls of a conquering army and without this heated crusading temper.

Let us begin by gratefully recognizing these facts. They are virtually a new feature in church history. The word "evangelism" has become an accepted part of our ecclesiastical vocabulary. We may use it now, without apology. The doors of some of our closed and stuffy churches have been flung open, and we breathe fresh air.

Even theologians—who in the past have been among the most unconquerable saboteurs of evangelism—seem to have rediscovered here and there its theological relevance. They realize that they jeopardize the Biblical authenticity of their thinking if they go on refusing to acknowledge that the church is set in this world with the sole purpose of carrying the gospel to the ends of the earth. In some schools of Protestant as well as of Roman Catholic theology, the apostolate tends to become the all-pervading center of thinking—a total revolution in theology, with overwhelmingly wide perspectives.

Nor is it only in the life of the older churches that evangelism has come to the fore again. In recent missionary thinking, we note the same consciousness of the necessity for a new advance. For almost forty years now we have smiled at the old ambitious plans to "evangelize the world in this generation," somewhat embarrassed and compassionate. Many of us have revised our judgment. Even so dignified a meeting as that of the International Missionary Council at Whitby in 1947 stated that such a thing might be possible, after all.[1]

And now we are questioned from both sides. The home base asks us what has become of our pioneer missionaries[2] and of the tenacious will of our missionary forefathers. There may, of course, be some romanticism behind the question. It is easier to get excited about a Christian bushranger than about a dignified pastor serving the church in another part of the world. But when, from the other side, some of the younger churches[3] ask where now are our "sacred fools"—those reckless gamblers with life, so well known in the past—there is some bitter realism in the question. The missionary-pioneer has become a rarity. Our work has become so institutionalized that mobility and spontaneity are hampered.

It is sad but true that even in the younger churches the second generation of Christians becomes established and immobile. And for a next generation, Christian life has often already become an unexciting business of routine. The call to evangelism is consequently as necessary there as anywhere else. All over the world, the necessity of leaving our safe church harbors and of putting to sea again is indelibly printed in our minds. And yet, if we listen carefully, we often hear other undertones as well. We discern a note of anxiety lest the church should lose face or be outrun by its powerful rivals. A glance through evangelistic pamphlets confronts one with words like "communistic menace," "Muslim expansion," or—recently—even the atom bomb.[4]

To put it bluntly: the call to evangelism is often little else than a call to restore "Christendom," the *Corpus Christianum,* as a solid, well-integrated cultural complex, directed and dominated by the church. And the sense of urgency is often nothing but a nervous feeling of insecurity, with the established church endangered; a flurried activity to save the remnants of a time now irrevocably past.

These are some of the undisclosed motives. In fact, the word "evangelize" often means a Biblical camouflage of what should rightly be called the reconquest of ecclesiastical influence. Hence this undue respect for statistics and this insatiable ecclesiastical hunger for ever more areas of life. We touch here upon one of the crucial problems of evangelism. We may approach it with a brief glance at the history of non-Roman Catholic evangelism.

Its main development coincided with the gradual break-down of Christendom. This was natural. The Reformers presupposed the existence of Christendom.[5] This is one of the reasons, no doubt, why they did not develop a full doctrine of the church. Their purpose was, not to create new communities, but to reform those already in existence. They have therefore reduced the number of distinctive marks of the true church to one: the proclamation of the Word in its double form: the verbal and sacramental Word.[6]

Later generations maintained this position, but meanwhile the face of society changed. The presupposed foundation of Christendom sank away, and we simply continued with our reduced ecclesiology. The sermon and the Sacraments were placed in a void, and often, to our astonishment, missed their reforming power, for in fact there was no community to be reformed.

The remarkable fact is that it was those very groups in which the springs of modern evangelism are to be found that were most keenly aware of the total transformation that had come over society. Both the Pietists and the Methodists protested violently against the spirit of the age. They realized that individualism completely lacked the spiritual setting for their work. Yet they continued as if they still lived in Christendom. They tried to isolate individuals and assemble them in an island of the saved, floating on a flood of perdition.

Later on, not even the French Revolution and the Revolution of 1848 were enough to open people's eyes and to make them realize that Christendom was past. One year, even, after the 1848 revolution—one year after the Communist Manifesto—Wichern, the father of home missions, spoke of the aim of evangelism as "winning back those people in Christendom who have become a prey to sin in such a way that the organized church no longer reaches them."[7]

This intimate relation between evangelism and an ideology of Christendom becomes even more clear as we look at missionary work. To assess realistically our present situation, we must try to disentangle the different motives. We will look at three examples:

1. Practice corrected theory very soon in pietistic missions. Only a few years after the death of Zinzendorf (1760), some of his Moravian brethren realized that they could not do effective work with their individualistic methods. Zinzendorf had instructed his missionaries to "gather individual souls" (*Seelen sammeln*) and "to stay away from all social and cultural work." Even schools were taboo.[8] The missionaries, however, discovered that their word needed a broad context. They tried to build up a form of what they called "Christian civilization" before they could begin to harvest the individual souls.[9]

2. Exactly one hundred years ago Missions-Inspector Karl Graul (1814–1864), of Leipzig, set out on his Indian tour. It became a decisive turning point in the development of evangelistic methods. In India, Graul became convinced that a person could not be converted unless his whole social context was Christianized at the same time. Hence *Volkschristianisierung* became as legitimate a part of evangelism as *Einzelbekehrung*.[10] Here again we find the intimate connection of Christendom and evangelism.

3. Suspect as they are, one may not neglect in this discussion the continuous stream of theologians in the nineteenth century from Schleiermacher to Troeltsch.[11] They stated with strong evidence that it would be impossible even to think of converting people without the simultaneous expansion of Western so-called Christian civilization, a point that was strongly put by Rothe: "One cannot make Christians with the Christian religion alone. Christian piety cannot be built in mid-air, but only on the foundation of christianized life."[12] It is clear that this point of view was an invitation to combine so-called Christian colonialism

with missions; and much of Anglo-Saxon missions would seem to fall in this same category, with highlights in the nineteenth century in the persons of Alexander Duff and David Livingstone.[13]

How do we stand today? Gradually we begin to realize that we cannot grasp the real situation on the basis of our traditional categories. We have discovered that Zinzendorf and his men were too much akin to rationalist individualism; that Graul was too much influenced by romanticism; that Warneck was too outspoken a nineteenth-century bourgeois;[14] and that Livingstone believed too firmly in the reality of the Christian character of Western civilization. They cannot guide us any longer, because they all believe, in one way or another, in the possible realization of the *Corpus Christianum,* and our experiences with this kind of Christendom have been too bitter for us to follow them any farther.

Moreover (and I am aware of the heresy I am now going to commit), the ecclesiology of the Reformers is too one-sided, too time-conditioned; it needs too much further extension and development for us to be able to follow them without hesitation or criticism. So we must look for another way.

There is yet another reason that forces us to do so. When we try to grasp what this coordination of Christendom and church really means, we see that almost without exception a number of Biblical concepts are distorted. I mention only three: the Biblical concepts of the church, of the heathen, and of salvation.

1. As regards the concept of the church, we see that in this way of thinking, Christendom becomes a protective shell of the church. The church tends to be built into the vast realm of Christian-influenced society. Christendom becomes a shock breaker. Influences from outside are filtered; condemnations hurled at the church are intercepted; in this well-protected area the church can have its

own style of life, speak its own language, determine its own
time. The direct intercourse between church and world has
ceased. The wolves are kept far from the little fold. A
splendid (very Christian-tinged) isolation is possible.
Life may change, but the church in this field of Christendom remains a bastion of the past, related to outworn
social structures.

2. In consequence, we have distorted the Biblical concept of the heathen. The church could see, from its safe
distance, two kinds of people. I will call them moral pagans
and intellectual pagans. Neither of them is conceived of
as heathen. That would be too shocking a statement. The
meaning of pagan is something quite different from
heathen. It means something like a backward man
(*paganus*), and this backwardness was generally located in
his moral behavior or in his intellectual privateering. The
drunkard and the skeptic have been the classical objects of
evangelism. And therefore, in general, our evangelistic
addresses have been either disgustingly moralistic or con-
descendingly apologetic. How deeply shocked we are, as
evangelists, even after realistic expositions of what life
without Christ must be, when we meet a man in total revolt
who completely rejects our message. Our *Corpus Christianum* ideology has made us forget what heathen really
are. In the safe environment of Christendom we could only
think of moral and intellectual pagans.

3. And again, in consequence of this view, we have the
distortion of the Biblical view of salvation. To the drunkard we offered salvation as a way to a better moral rearma-
ment, to the skeptic we offered wisdom. For the one, the
forgiveness of sins meant ignoring a wild past; for the
other, overlooking stupidity.

And now we realize, gradually, what an impossible outlook this has been. The world has come to the church's
doorstep. The heathen can no longer—for our relief—be
disguised as a moral or an intellectual pagan. And we are

aware of the alarming fact that, after our moralistic advice and intellectual enlightenment, we have not proclaimed salvation, but have offered stones for bread.

If this analysis has any truth in it, the call to evangelism finds us unprepared. The ecumenical inquiry on evangelism begins by confessing that to many questions the only possible answer is, "We do not know." But we do know that we cannot continue as before. We need a new vision of evangelism, a disentanglement of all secular complexes and secret ideologies—a recovery, in short, of the Biblical sense of evangelism.

Throughout the Bible, the evangelization of the heathen is seen as a possibility only in the Messianic days.[15] In the Old Testament it is the Messiah who gathers the nations. "Unto him shall the gathering of the people be" (Gen. 49:10). His will to save becomes so powerful that all resistance is overcome. "In the last days," i.e., in the days of the Messiah, the nations will come and praise God. In other words: the Messiah is the evangelist. Only to his power and his authority will men surrender.

It is written of the Son of Man (Dan. 7:13–14) that "there was given him dominion, and glory, and a kingdom, that all people . . . should serve him." In the New Testament we find this same context. Jesus dies without having given the explicit order to carry the promises of the gospel beyond the limits of Israel. Only after the resurrection, after the Messiah has revealed himself in his power, victorious even over death, is the way to the heathen made free. The great commission in Matt., ch. 28, is a reference to Dan., ch. 7. Now, after the resurrection, *now* only, Jesus says, "All power is given unto me in heaven and in earth. Go therefore and make all heathen my disciples."[16] Now the last days have dawned on you, you have entered the Messianic era, now you walk in the midst of the signs of coming glory. You are transplanted in the aeon where you live in the fellowship of the Kingdom which is to come.[17] And one of the decisive signs of the time, a token that the end is imminent—and yet some time *still* is given—is that the gospel of the Kingdom shall be preached in all the world for a witness to all heathen, and then shall the end come (cf. Matt. 24:14). This eschatological perspective has been one of the constant elements in our missionary thinking for a long time.[18] Two of the obvious consequences thereof have, however, only very seldom been drawn.

The first is that the Messiah (i.e., the Christ) is the subject of evangelism. Paul expresses this conviction in his epistles to the Corinthians, showing that the apostles can march only as conquered men in the triumphal procession of God (II Cor. 2:14).

The second consequence is that the aim of evangelism can be nothing less than what Israel expected the Messiah to do, i.e., he will establish the shalom. And shalom is much more than personal salvation.[19] It is at once peace, integrity, community, harmony, and justice. Its rich content can be felt in Ps. 85, where we read that shalom is there, where "mercy and truth are met together; righteousness and peace have kissed each other. Truth shall spring out of the earth; and righteousness shall look down from heaven."

The Messiah is the prince of shalom (Isa. 9:6), he shall be the shalom (Micah 5:5), he shall speak shalom unto the heathen (Zech. 9:10); or, in the prophecy of Jeremiah (ch. 29:11), he will realize the plans of shalom, which the Lord has in mind for us, to give us a future and hope.

In the New Testament, God's shalom is the most elementary expression of what life in the new aeon actually is.[20] Jesus leaves shalom with his disciples—"Shalom I leave with you, my shalom I give unto you" (John 14:27), and the preaching of the apostles is summarized as "preaching shalom through Jesus Christ" (Acts 10:36; cf. Isa. 52:7). "We are ambassadors therefore on behalf of Christ, . . . working together with him" to proclaim "now is the day of shalom" (II Cor. 5:20; 6:1–2).

This concept in all its comprehensive richness should be our leitmotiv in Christian work. God intends the redemption of the whole of creation. He must reign until he has put all his enemies under his feet. In some segments of creation his sovereignty may be established already: shalom for all life; destruction of all solitude, obliteration of all injustice, "to give men a future and hope." Is this a utopian ideal? Or could it be apocalyptic realism? A superhuman task? Or is this the marching on of the victorious Son of Man? Is it not possible in what Dr. Minear has described as the *modus vivendi* of the new age—"the mood of expectant wonder, of ecstatic joy, of buoyant confidence"?[21] These are the kinds of questions we must answer before we can deal with problems of evangelistic method.

Evangelism can be nothing but the realization of hope, a function of expectancy. Throughout the history of the church, wherever this hope became once more the dominant note of Christian life, an outburst of evangelistic zeal followed. That should make us think, surrounded as we are by clamant calls to evangelism.

In *The Truth of Vision,* Dr. Warren writes:

Any effective prosecution of the Church's primary task of evangelism in the world of our time must surely depend upon the nature of its hope. Incidentally, and as a corollary to that, we need to note that the nature of the hope will largely determine the character of evangelism.[22]

This Messianic conception of evangelism means a total rejection of two very well-known methods:

1. It means in the first place a total rejection of everything that tends to be propaganda.[23] I take this word in the meaning and with the content given to it by Martin Kähler, who distinguished very sharply between missions and propaganda. He clarified this distinction once in the image used by Paul in I Cor., ch. 15, where we read (vs. 36 ff.): "That which thou thyself sowest is not quickened,

except it die: . . . thou sowest not that body that shall be, but bare grain. . . . But God giveth it a body as it hath pleased him, and to every seed his own body." To evangelize is to sow and wait in respectful humility and in expectant hope: in humility, because the seed that we sow has to die; in hope, because we expect that God will quicken this seed and give it its proper body.

In propaganda, however, we imagine that we sow the body that will be. Propaganda's essential character is a lack of expectant hope and an absence of due humility. The propagandist has to impose himself. He has to resort to himself, to his word (verbosity being a characteristic of every propagandist). In short, the propagandist tries to make exact copies of himself. (*Er macht Wiederholungen, dessen was man selbst ist.*) He attempts to make man in his image and after his likeness.

It is not difficult to make this distinction in theory. It is, however, one of our most painful and most frequent experiences that evangelism is almost always concealed in a form of propaganda. Be it ever so lowly, through our witness of shalom, there sounds also a call: Follow me!

For example, do we really hope, and can we really expect, that God can give another than a Lutheran, or a Reformed, or an Anglican body to the seed that we sow? Do we not act as if God has thought out already all forms in which he may shape his shalom? And is not this confessional propaganda almost without exception the form in which our evangelization is concealed?

To let Christian hope determine our evangelism means that we move forward in a world with unlimited possibilities, a world in which we shall not be surprised when something unforeseen happens, but shall, rather, be really surprised at our little faith, which forbids us to expect the unprecedented.

2. In the second place, the Messianic conception of evangelism also means a complete rejection of another frequent misconception of evangelism. There is a stub-

born tradition in our midst that interprets the aim of evangelism as the planting of the church (or even the extension of the church). This tradition has a respectable past. In the seventeenth century, Voetius defined as the aim of missions the *plantatio ecclesiae*.[24] It is certain that he borrowed this conception from Roman Catholicism, but it is one that has been adopted by many since. I am sure that many of us hold it.

What happens here is that missions are seen as the road from the church to the church. It is the outgoing activity of one church—it can remain as it was before—to a place in the world where again a church is planted. In principle, the task of missions is completed as soon as this church exists, in the same way as in Roman Catholic circles missions must withdraw as soon as the hierarchy is created.

It is possible to justify this position. But we should be aware of a temptation to take the church itself too seriously, to invite the church to see itself as well-established, as God's secure bridgehead in the world, to think of itself as a *beatus possidens* which, having what others do not have, distributes its possession to others, until a new company of *possidentes* is formed.

We reach here a crucial issue. It is common to think of evangelism, to think of the apostolate, as a function of the church. *Credo ecclesiam apostolicam* is often interpreted as: "I believe in the church, which has an apostolic function." Would it not be truer to make a complete turnover here, and to say that this means: I believe in the church, which is a function of the apostolate, that is, an instrument of God's redemptive action in this world. Or to put it in terms we used here, the church is (nothing more, but also nothing less!) a means in God's hands to establish shalom in this world. It is taken into the triumphal procession of the glorified Son of Man, and on its way it discovers that it walks amid the tokens of the coming Kingdom. And, if this statement has any truth in it, it is also true that planting the church in this institutional way of thinking cannot be the aim of missions. Evangelism and *churchification* are not identical, and very often they are each other's bitterest enemies.

When Christian hope, the partaking of the coming Kingdom, has really to determine the character of our evangelism, it is impossible to think of the *plantatio ecclesiae* as the end of evangelism. It is too poor a conception and betrays too clearly a lack of expectant hope. It is too static a view of the church as a closed and definitive entity.

If, now, we try to find the right translation of Messianic shalom, we may take as our starting point Matt., ch. 9. Jesus is asked there: Are you he that should come? That is, are you really the Messiah, who will establish his shalom? The answer is: "Go and show . . . those things which ye do hear and see: The blind receive their sight, . . . the lepers are cleansed, and the deaf hear, the dead are raised up, and the poor have the gospel preached to them." This is the Messianic shalom in its abundant multiplicity.

1. This shalom is *proclaimed*. That is one aspect of evangelism. In the kerygma, that shalom is represented in the literal sense, it is made present.

2. This shalom is *lived*. That is another aspect of evangelism. It is lived in koinonia. We must not speak too quickly of community. Only insofar as men are partakers of the shalom, represented in the kerygma, do they live in mutual communion and fellowship.

3. There is a third aspect of evangelism. This shalom is *demonstrated* in humble service, diakonia. To partake of the shalom in koinonia means practically and realistically to act as a humble servant. Whosoever will be great among you shall be your servant. And whosoever will be the chiefest shall be servant of all (Mark 10:43 f.).

These three aspects, kerygma, koinonia, and diakonia, should be integrated in our work of evangelism. Only so, are our methods of evangelism justified.

The kerygma is the proclamation that the shalom has come. Christ is there. We have not to look for another. We have entered upon the last days of total renewal. But, with the kerygma alone, in isolation, the evangelist soon becomes a more or less interesting orator. He needs the manifestation of the koinonia of which he is a part, and he has to justify himself as a witness of the Messiah-Servant in his diakonia.

The koinonia manifests the shalom, as it is present among men. But we need the continuous reminder of the kerygma, the interpretation of this shalom as the salvation of the Messiah, and the diakonia should prevent this shalom from being used in a self-sufficient way.

The diakonia translates the shalom into the language of humble service. But if we isolate this diakonia or give it an undue emphasis, then the evangelist soon becomes a sentimental philanthropist. He must never forget that he cannot render real service if he deprives man of the kerygma and leaves him outside the koinonia.

It is a remarkable fact that the call for evangelism is now, in so many parts of the world, a call for this comprehensive evangelism.[25] In this respect missions would seem to be far ahead of the older churches' areas. But there is a *rapprochement*. We should not overlook the fact that evangelistic work in Europe, for example, is beginning to acknowledge the need to learn of missionary methods. In the Netherlands, articles on rural evangelism contain frequent references to the missionary work in so-called primitive areas in Indonesia. In France, the Roman Catholic priests have taken as the pattern for their work in the industrial sub-proletariat the great missionary to Muslims, de Foucauld. In fact, one religious order, les Filles du Père Foucauld, has two branches, one working among the Muslims in North Africa and one among the industrial workers in Marseilles. In both branches they use in principle the same method. It is therefore neither new, nor followed in only half the world.

Let us try to study these three aspects somewhat more precisely.

1. Professor Dodd has shown that the apostolic preaching, the kerygma, was strictly objective.[26] For this history of God's great acts there was apparently no point of contact in our life. We cannot use our own experiences to interpret or to clarify what God has done. There is a notable lack of personal stories in the apostolic preaching. It is constantly affirmed that in the kerygma a history is proclaimed, of which all men are ignorant until it is announced as a revelation, things that "eye hath not seen, nor ear heard, neither have entered into the heart of man" (I Cor. 2:9). All witness that neglects or minimizes this character of revelation is useless, for it is disobedient and unfaithful.

This point should be emphasized, for it is precisely in evangelistic work that we run the risk of minimizing this feature of revelation. The temptation to mask the mystery, to avoid the scandal of the gospel, becomes almost inevitable, once we are confronted with men who are perplexed by the absurdity of our message. We tend, then, to reduce the gospel to a few vague religious generalities, or the propagandist awakens in us, and we try to impose ourselves, with our personal experiences, which are obviously irrefutable. And through a false fidelity to the man before us, we tend to become unfaithful to Christ, who has committed unto us the proclamation of this scandalous, mysterious gospel.

This said, something else should be added. This fidelity is quite different from any kind of rigidity. The representation of shalom is something quite different from a precise enumeration of all the shibboleths of orthodoxy. Merle Davis has recently given a remarkable example of this rigid proclamation.

In Madagascar, after a generation of proclaiming Jesus as the Lamb of God who sits on the right hand of His Throne and whose blood alone can save from sin, the old chief of a tribe which has resisted the Christian message revealed the reason for his people's indifference. "We are a cattle-raising people; we despise sheep. Our clans asked the early missionaries whether there was a place on God's throne for a cow as well as for a sheep and when they were told 'no' they closed their hearts to the Christian Gospel."[27]

Any of us could enlarge on these examples. The hearers are not shocked by the fact that the message is incomprehensible, but they are scandalized by this inflexibility, by the fact that a man who has to proclaim freedom to the prisoners himself remains a prisoner. The gospel is not merely glad tidings to him, but rather, an ideology, to which he has to submit himself. That is why he repeats himself. The kerygma becomes a stereotyped recital, unrelated to the world where it is proclaimed. And so he tells the blind that the lame walk, and the lame that the blind receive their sight. To the bourgeois he bears witness to the shalom for the proletariat, and to the proletarians he gives a message in which they can recognize nothing but a bourgeois shalom.

To regain liberty and flexibility in our witness two things must happen: We must in the first place find ourselves fully at home in this strange new world of the Bible so that we can move familiarly about and concretize and articulate the shalom in a different way in different situations. And secondly, as the Reverend D. T. Jenkins puts it, we must

be aware, from within, of the situation which the Gospel addresses in our own time. . . . We must strive to understand the whole religious, moral and intellectual setting in which people are placed. . . . Even those who appear most indifferent to the vital currents of thought going on in the world around them, and who certainly cannot understand them, come to sense after a time that the situation is different from what it used to be and adjust themselves accordingly. One of the reasons for the irrelevance of the Church's proclamation in recent times has been that it has been content to achieve communication on too narrow a front. We have expressed our Gospel too narrowly in terms of the conscious experience of the middle-class people in our pews, forgetting that even they lived in a world where they were being unconsciously exposed to movements of thought very different from those which they themselves would naturally frame.[28]

2. The koinonia is the place where the shalom is already lived. As such, the Christian community belongs to the new age. That means that this fellowship of the partakers of the same salvation is nothing more in this world than a company of strangers and pilgrims (I Peter 2:11), a paroikia, or group of sojourners in the world, fully detached and therefore free to relate itself to every form of existence.

The Christian community, therefore, is (or should be) an open community, open to everyone who has become a partaker of the same shalom. In practice this is not the case. In an unconscious way the national churches have become closed, because they related Christian community and nationality too exclusively, and in the West the churches have become class churches, because they identified themselves too uncritically with one special group of society. It is nonsense to call these churches to evangelism, if we do not call them simultaneously to a radical revision of their life and a revolutionary change of their structure.

It is here that we are confronted in Europe with some of the most ardent problems of evangelism. When evangelists come together, one of their main topics of discussion is sure to be the creation of extra-church communities, groups serving as meeting—and mediating—centers between church and world.[29] It may be necessary to create them as an interim measure. But we should realize that as soon as these halfway communities between church and world become a permanent feature, we have in fact given up hope for the church. We conceive of it then as a body definitive and static, over against the world as the other static entity. And this is nothing less than to despair of establishing shalom in the church and of realizing the koinonia.

Another complex of questions lies in the field of the relation of existing human groups to the koinonia. As soon as we say that the koinonia is an open community, we imply that it can be realized in a variety of social structures. We deplore the breakdown of the primary social groups (family, neighborhood, etc.) in modern mass society. But at the same time many of us continue as if these were still the basic units. Koinonia, however, is so flexible that the unity of the modern city quarter, of the factory, of the trade-union or of the communist cell can be related to shalom (though this does not mean, of course, that these groups are thereby accepted). Some experiments have been made in this field. The work of the Roman Catholic priests among workers in France (for example in Marseilles) is directed toward the three contexts of the industrial worker's life—his factory, his living quarters, and his pub fellowship.[30]

The main and all-decisive function of the koinonia is, however, that it is the primary kerygmatic and diakonic unit, kerygmatic as the place where the shalom is really made present, diakonic because it has no other relation to the outside world than that of humble service. It is here that the call to evangelism becomes of biting actuality. It is no use stimulating to new and rapid advance while this work remains neutralized by the mockery of koinonia that our churches really are. "The acts of your koinonia speak so loudly that we cannot hear the words of your kerygma."

3. And finally, confronted with a state that sets out to care for man from the cradle to the grave, one has the feeling that the diakonia will be reduced on the one hand to charity, which is the diakonia of Matt., ch. 25: Give the thirsty to drink and clothe the naked; and on the other hand to prophecy, the service that one renders in accom-

panying life with the message of divine judgment, putting a lamp unto the feet, a light unto the path of the state (the diakonia of Ps. 119). [31] For this reason people outside the church see it both as a philanthropic agency, a body that escapes the fight for justice in condescending charity, and as a "factory for solemn statements."

There is, however, a third possibility, through which we can avoid this constant temptation to the church to speak when it should act. We may call it the level of the laboratory, the diakonia of a little group, living in a concrete situation, and serving each other and their environment by reforming the structure of a segment of society. Social problems are not solved at this level, but life is made more tolerable. The opposition to the Messianic shalom is not completely broken, but here and there it is tempered. It is not the Kingdom of God that is constructed, but some significant tokens are set up. An object lesson is given of what shalom should be. (25.)

II

THE CHURCH IN PERSPECTIVE

WHEN THE BIBLE SPEAKS of Messianic fulfillment the key issue is the Kingdom for the *world*. This is fundamental. Everything that wants to be more than an interpretation of this one little sentence might actually turn out to be less.

The exalted Lord, who in and through his own coming has brought the Kingdom "at hand," has also opened the doors to the world. The "world" as correlate of the "Kingdom" is a Messianic concept. The ends of the earth and the end of time belong together. Eschatology and universality are both dimensions of the Messianic fullness. And this is the meaning of our history, that until the end of time the ends of the earth, the whole oikoumene, are confronted with the Kingdom (Matt. 24:14).[1] (32, 153–154.)

It is striking that the New Testament speaks about mission as a postulate of eschatology,[2] and that from a threefold perspective: the apocalyptic, the redemptive-historical, and the apostolic. In this connection we can present only a brief outline.

1. In the *apocalyptic* passages, mission is mentioned as one of the signs of the times. Where there is talk about wars, famine, cosmic catastrophes, persecutions, and the antichrist, there mission to the Gentiles too is mentioned as a signal of the end, indicating how far advanced in age the world actually is.

Mark 13:10 (par.): "The gospel must (the *dei* of the eschatological necessity) first be preached to all nations"; this gospel of the Kingdom will be preached to *panta ta ethnē* (i.e., those whose hatred one must endure for Jesus' sake, v. 9) as a testimony (*marturion*) (Matt. 24:14).

These words receive their commentary elsewhere in the Scriptures. Followed by war, famine, and death, the triumphant gospel spreads across the earth (Rev. 6:1–8); the preachers of penitence of the end time (Moses and Elijah) must first preach the gospel to *panta ta ethnē* (Rev. 11:3; cf. Lohmeyer), and a last appeal is made to every nation, tongue, and people, "for the hour of his judgment has come" (Rev. 14:6–7).

Cullmann now finds the same combination of ideas in the mysterious words of II Thess. 2:6–7. In the unfolding of the plan just before the last stage of history, the manifestation of the Antichrist is held back (*katechein*) on account of the preaching to the nations.

The walls of history are held apart, as it were, through the church's mission. The end is imminently near. The mission to the nations witnesses to this. That the end has not yet come, that we are given time, and that in an incomprehensible patience there is also given the *kairoi tou ethnou,* that is the great miracle which qualifies the history that precedes the end. "If history still continues, then that is singularly because the gospel for the world must first be announced to all the nations. The history of the world has from now on no other significance."[3]

Here one finds the basic elements for a Biblical "philosophy" of history, a realm of inquiry which already so frequently has been associated with the church's mission.[4]

2. Thus we have made the transition to the aspect of *redemptive history*. In the missionary command several motifs are gathered together which give a further explication of this aspect.[5]

The great commission (Matt. 28:19) is inserted between a Messianic declaration of power (v. 18) and a promise of the Holy Spirit (v. 20). In v. 18 we see Dan. 7:13–14 come into fulfillment. The dominion, the glory, and the Kingdom have now truly been given to the Son of Man; now peoples, nations, and languages shall serve him. The service of the nations is thus part of the enthronement of the Son of Man.

Prophecy has been supremely fulfilled. "To the Son of Man has been given *all* power in heaven and on earth." No longer are there powers and dominions besides those which have already been subjected to him. The triumphal entry of the Son of Man, who will come in glory (Matt. 16:27; 26:64), has already been initiated. And this enthronement must be proclaimed (Matt. 28:19). In this proclamation the exalted Messiah will be present through the Spirit, until this age, which has been inaugurated with Christ's exaltation, has finished its course (v. 20b).

Three motifs, which will return repeatedly, are interrelated here. The imperative of the apostolate rests upon the two indicatives of the Messianic fulfillment and the promise of the Spirit. We will have to enter a little more deeply into each one of these motifs.

The conversion of the Gentiles is a *Messianic* event. "In the last days," *panta ta ethnē* will turn to Yahweh (Isa. 2:2, LXX). This is nothing less than a Messianic miracle, the eschatological dealings of Yahweh himself, who comes to judge the nations.[6]

"The spread of the belief in Yaweh is the miracle act of Yaweh himself. It takes place without historical foundation or mediation, and belongs for this reason within the context of the eschatological expectations."[7] Cf. Isa. 2:2–4 (Micah 4:1–3); Isa. 11:10; 25:6–8; Jer. 16:19; Zech. 8:20–23; 14:14; etc.

All this is in accordance with the Old Testament eschatology, in which judgment (*mishpat*) upon the nations constitutes a solid ingredient. "Mishpat has become a comprehensive designation of the revelation of Yaweh in which the relationship of Yaweh to his chosen people was set, and which also constitutes his relationship to the nations." Sellin renders it as *Gottesherrschaft* (divine rule).[8]

In Deutero-Isaiah this basic eschatological thought of the conversion of the nations has been worked out extensively. Now that the end time has arrived, the national boundaries no longer form a barrier to redemption. In the Messianic oikoumene the light enlightens the nations. "As far as Deutero-Isaiah is concerned, the earth and mankind who inhabits it form one whole (chs. 40:4; 42:5; 45:6, 18). In the now-initiated end time it will once again be as it was in the days of Creation. From sunrise till sunset the nations will behold all the dealings of the God who has created them; they will hear all the words which the Lord addresses to them (chs. 41; 43:9; 45:20; 28:14; 51:4).

"When the Lord of heaven establishes his righteousness somewhere upon the earth, it radiates forth from there, and it resounds across all national barriers until the ends of the earth. And when the nations hear it, they either go up to the place where the divine voice sounds forth (chs. 45:15; 55:4), or they simply pray from their own lands to the new King who has revealed himself to them through his Word or through his arm, i.e., his deeds, and they honor him (chs. 42:10–12; 45:6 f.; 22 ff.; 51:4–6)."[9]

In the "Ebed-Yahweh songs" also one finds these same ideas (this contra Volz, who wishes to see a transition of the mission idea to the mission deed in chs. 42 and 49).

This "eschatological universalism" becomes historicized in the LXX. "The eschatological expectation of the conversion of the Gentiles seems to appear here as lying within historical reach. Cf. LXX, Isa. 18:7; 55:5; Jer. 3:19."[10]

It was known in Judaism as well that the real mission would not start until the days of Messiah or at the time of the last judgment. The rabbis have almost without exception interpreted the word of the Psalmist, "all kneel before him" (Ps. 22:29) as the appearance of all people before the judgment seat of God.[11]

This cluster of ideas is of special importance because of the manner in which the New Testament sees these Messianic prophecies fulfilled, as in, for instance, Isa. 45:20–24, in

Rom. 14:11 (the last day) and Phil. 2:11 (honor to the exalted Christ in the congregation). "A word of invitation (Isa. 45:23) has become a summons (Rom. 14:11). In Phil. 2:10 f., however, the same formula is applied to the exalted *kurios.*"[12]

This perspective determines to a large measure also the missionary approach in the New Testament. For example, Jesus' attitude toward the mission to the Gentiles cannot be described as a progressively developing universalism. The contrast between particularism and universalism cannot legitimately be applied to either the Old Testament or the New Testament. Redemption for the Gentiles is prepared precisely in the concentration of the messianic work among Israel (cf. Deutero-Isaiah).

This has been demonstrated quite convincingly, although one-sidedly, by B. Sundkler.[13] Jesus considers himself sent exclusively to the lost sheep of Israel (Matt. 15:24). When Israel rejects him, he does not turn to the Gentiles, but travels the Via Dolorosa. "He could not abandon Israel, for he was the Son (the Son of Man who was the Son of David). And it was the mission of the Son to make the remnant of Israel into the house and the people of Israel. Jesus was a Jew, and that in this particularistic sense. Jesus was convinced that the central point, the meaning and the end of the history of redemption was the salvation of Israel. In the meantime, that did not exclude the mission among the Gentiles. Quite to the contrary, only from this point of departure does mission become possible. 'Do not depart from Jerusalem' (Acts 1:14), *thus* the world will be saved."[14] This interpretation has met with substantial agreement as far as its main emphasis is concerned, and in my judgment it must be considered correct.[15]

Only after the rejection of the Messiah by Israel, after the cross and the resurrection, does the exalted Christ open the way to the Gentiles. Consequently, in the book of The Acts the mission to the Gentiles occurs repeatedly, because of the rejection of the Messiah by Israel. God's great plan of redemption thus finds its concrete expression in these *Heilsgeschichtliche* tactics through which the apostles turn from the synagogue to the nations.[16] Finally, Paul has placed the mission to the Gentiles in its redemptive-historical context: it is the divinely offered possibility between the Fall and the restoration of Israel (Rom., chs. 9 to 11).[17]

The other motifs that we found in Matt. 28:18–20 are indicated by H. Schlier when he summarizes: "There is only mission to the Gentiles on the presupposition that Jesus the Messiah has been risen from the dead and has been elevated to the right hand of God, has given his Holy Spirit and sent his apostles."[18] Thus the pneumatic and apostolic aspects of the mission to the Gentiles are pointed out.

The gift of the Spirit is a presupposition of the mission to the Gentiles. The preaching of the gospel to the ends of the earth is specifically made dependent on the reception of the Spirit (Acts 1:8; cf. Luke 24:49). The whole book of The Acts witnesses to this. It is always again the Spirit who must overcome resistances and must drive the church out to the Gentiles. "The pneumatic apostolate is apostolate to the Gentiles."[19]

The motifs that (taking our starting point in Matt. 28:18–20) we have linked together here occur in an incomparably clear combination in Luke 24:46 f.: there we find them together as aspects of God's redemptive plan with mankind: the suffering and the resurrection of the Messiah (v. 46), the preaching to the Gentiles (v. 47), and the promise of the Spirit (v. 49). "Thus it is written." (V. 46.)

When we now combine this *Heilsgeschichtliche* aspect with the apocalyptic one, we can summarize this section as follows: Mission to the Gentiles is the divinely given possibility, which is rooted in the reality of the fulfillment of the Messianic promise concerning the conversion of the "nations." It takes place in these "last days," the time between the exaltation and the return of Christ; it is part of the eschatological acts of God, by means of which he executes his redemptive plan and, through his Spirit, ever anew overcomes our resistance and unwillingness, and thus drives the gospel into the whole oikoumene. "Holy Spirit and mission are the marks of the end phase in which we live, and which is qualified by the future."[20]

3. All the above themes recur in the Biblical notion of the *apostolate*. Apocalyptic (II Thess. 2:6 f.), redemptive-historical, and pneumatic motifs are here intertwined.[21] Only in the "last days," i.e., after the exaltation of the Messiah, can there be any question of the apostolate in the strict sense of the word. All preceding missions were temporary and of a local nature. "In the universality of the mission lies the 'plus' of the renewed, final authorization of the Twelve by the resurrected Lord, over against the pre-Easter apostolate."[22] The apostles are the messengers of the end time, announcers of the approaching day of the Lord (Isa. 52:7, cited in Rom. 10:13–19), men who proclaim the fulfillment of the Messianic promises (Isa. 49:8, cited in II Cor. 6:1–2).[23]

When Paul calls himself the "apostle to the Gentiles," he does not merely make a practical distinction with respect to the apostolate among the Jews, but he applies a designation which refers to the eschatological and redemptive-historical dealings of God.

The apostle Paul's designation as apostle to the Gentiles has an eschatological, not a practical basis, and inasmuch as his call to become an apostle to the nations coincides with that eschatological outlook, it consequently justifies the fact that the gospel must first be preached to the gentiles (Rom., chs. 9 to 11). The limit of this task is precisely its limitlessness; among all the nations, that will be its eschatological outcome. When this task is completed, the end will be![24]

Fridrichsen states it differently, but similarly as to content:

The apostle is to stand in the center of the eschatological development between the resurrection and return of the Messiah.[25]

It is true that the apostolate retains a relative independence beside the gift of the Spirit insofar as it is instituted in a separate and preceding act (Matt. 28:18 ff.; Luke 24:47 ff.; Acts 1:6 ff.; John 20:21 f.)[26]; nevertheless, apostolate and Spirit are always so intimately related (John 20:21 f.) that Paul eventually can speak of his apostolate as *diakonia tou pneumatos* (II Cor. 3:8).

The Spirit incorporates the apostle into God's plan of redemption. His own plans are repeatedly crossed through instructions by the Spirit (e.g., Acts 16:6 ff.). Paul lives under divine compulsion (I Cor. 9:16), and when he resists this leading, he is still carried along in the divine triumphant procession as a captive. "The whole mission is a triumphal procession of God in which Paul marches along as a conquered opponent." (II Cor. 2:12 ff.)[27]

Thus the apostle becomes an instrument in God's eschatological plan, the mysteries of which are revealed by the Spirit. The apostolate, the divine oikonomia, and the mysterion among the heathen can be mentioned in one breath (Col. 1:22–29). "Thus the destiny of the world is dependent on the mission to the gentiles and also on the apostle to the gentiles. Through the apostle Christ leads the world to its end."[28] (11, 223–228.)

Various things must now receive their proper place within this general framework, which can here only be indicated in a few sketchy lines. One can be absolutely certain that the mentioning of the series: Kingdom—apostolate—oikoumene will immediately evoke a response that contains a passionate plea for the church.[29] It is feared that church life will evaporate in a restless sequence of actions. We fear the loss of ecclesiastical substance when the "event" is not immediately accompanied by the "institution,"[30] and when the Word on its journey through the lands cannot come to rest in fellowship (koinonia) around the Sacraments.

It is true that the context Kingdom—apostolate—oikoumene does not leave much room for the church. Ecclesiology does not fit here. When one desires to speak about God's dealings with the world, the church can be mentioned only in passing and without strong emphasis. Ecclesiology cannot be more than a single paragraph from Christology (the *Messianic* dealings with the world) and a few sentences from eschatology (the Messianic dealings with the *World*). The church is only the church to the extent that she lets herself be used as a part of God's dealings with the oikoumene. For this reason she can only be "ecumenical," i.e., oriented toward the oikoumene—the whole world (32, 154).

Church-centric missionary thinking is bound to go astray, because it revolves around an illegitimate center. To say that "the church is the starting point and the goal of the mission" is only to make a phenomenological statement. The church-centrism, which apparently is the only undisputed missiological dogma since Jerusalem in 1928, has such a grasp on us that we don't even notice anymore how our thinking has become completely "ecclesiasticized." It may well be that we are so wrapped up in our church centrism that we hardly realize any longer how much our ideas are open to controversy. Would it not be a good thing to start all over again and try to understand what it really means when we quote and requote our favorite missionary text, "The gospel of the Kingdom will be proclaimed throughout the oikoumene"—attempting to re-think our ecclesiology within this framework of Kingdom-gospel-apostolate-world?

In the New Testament, oikoumene stands for "the communion of the heathen, . . . mankind destined to perish, . . . which, in its utter self-confidence, stands apposed to the gospel."[31] For this oikoumene the Kingdom is destined; world (kosmos/oikoumene) and Kingdom are correlated to each other; the world is conceived of as a unity, the scene of God's great acts: it is the *world* which has been reconciled (II Cor. 5:19), the *world* which God loves (John 3:16) and which he has overcome in his love (John 16:33); the *world* is the field in which the seeds of the Kingdom are sown (Matt. 13:38)—the world is consequently the scene for the proclamation of the Kingdom.

Let us not try to narrow this sphere. What justification is there for the traditional policy of our churches in which this one apostolic task is carefully divided as the one (primary) task on this side of political/linguistic frontiers and the other task beyond these frontiers; how can we make a theologically relevant distinction between home and foreign missions (or evangelism and missions)? *Kingdom and world belong together.* The kerygma of the early Christians did not know of a redemptive act of God that was not directed toward the whole world. There can be no question about it: in the New Testament the world-as-a-unity is confronted with the Kingdom.[32]

The Kingdom, destined for the whole pagan rebellious world (oikoumene), must be announced to this world. It is of the essence of the *gospel* that it be proclaimed, just as it is an essential part of the reconciliation that the "ministry of reconciliation" is instituted (II Cor. 5:18). God's great acts can only be actualized, represented through proclamations. Announcing the gospel, therefore, is an essential part of the gospel itself.[33]

Thus the gospel and the apostolate belong intrinsically together. Through the apostolate the gospel comes to "fulfillment" (Rom. 15:19; cf. Col. 1:24) and is brought to its destination. In the apostolate, God continues to struggle with the world for the sake of the world. Its *subject* is "the apostle Jesus" (Heb. 3:1); the "deeds of Christ" (Matt. 11:2) are continued in the apostolic "work of the Lord" (I Cor. 15:58; 16:10). The *realm* of the apostolate is the oikoumene; the *substance* of the apostolate is the setting up of signs of Kingdom-salvation, i.e., shalom; the apostolate is carried out in kerygma (i.e., representation of shalom through proclamation), in koinonia (corporate participation of shalom), and in diakonia (demonstration of shalom, by way of humble service).[34]

Where in this context does the *church* stand? Certainly not at the starting point, nor at the end. The church has no fixed place at all in this context, it *happens* insofar as it actually proclaims the Kingdom to the world. The church has no other existence than *in actu Christi,* that is, *in actu Apostoli.* Consequently it cannot be firmly established but will always remain the paroikia, a temporary settlement which can never become a permanent home. The real autochthony of the church, the soil in which it should be rooted, is the foundation of the apostles and prophets. Only insofar as the church shares in the mission of the apostles, only insofar as it is on the way toward the ends of the earth and the end of time, does it remain "autochthonous." We should therefore not only consider the Old Testament *qahal* as the antetype of the Christian church; Christ is not merely a new Moses, he is the Second Adam (Rom. 5:14; I Cor. 15:22, 45). His body is not a new religious community, but the coming into being of a new mankind (Eph. 2:14 ff.). Both the Son of Man and the Servant of God are destined to save *hoi polloi,* the whole of mankind.

Whatever else can be said about the church may be of only little relevance. The *nature* of the church can be sufficiently defined by its *function,* i.e., its participation in Christ's apostolic ministry. To proclaim the gospel of the Kingdom throughout the oikoumene is the church's *opus proprium,* in fact, it is not her work at all but *ergon Kyriou.*[35] "The church can exist only to the extent that it is the mission," says Elert.[36] To put it differently, it lives only insofar as it partakes actively in the "economy of witness," which Christianity signifies in the New Testament.[37] (37, 8–11.)

The church lives for the world. She can only "share in the gospel" if she desires to serve all (I Cor. 9:19–23).

Whether a church really has apostolic substance will always become apparent in her diakonia, in her *servant* form. On the other hand, the church can only really be the church if she is a sign and prophetic witness of the approaching Kingdom. In her *existence* she will establish the sign of the redemption of God's Kingdom: communion, righteousness, unity, etc. The church cannot be more than a sign. She points away from herself to the Kingdom; she lets herself be used for and through the Kingdom in the oikoumene. There is nothing that the church can demand for herself and can possess for herself (not an ecclesiology either). God has placed her in a living relationship to the Kingdom and to the oikoumene. The church exists only *in actu,* in the execution of the apostolate, i.e., in the proclamation of the gospel of the Kingdom to the world.

Everything that has been said up till now could be summarized as follows: *The church is a function of the apostolate*. We want to illustrate this thesis by means of two examples:

1. From this perspective on the nature and the task of the church, it becomes impossible to distinguish in principle between mission and oikoumene. In no way can *mission* be viewed as *one* among other tasks to which the church is called. A church that knows that she is a function of the apostolate and that her very ground of existence lies in the proclamation of the Kingdom to the world, does not engage in missions, but she herself *becomes* mission, she becomes the living outreach of God to the world. That is why a church without mission is an absurdity. As soon as the church fails to become mission in the totality of

her being, she thereby proves that she has been denatural-
ized into a temple or into some sort of association for the
cultivation of one's personal religious life.

The oikoumene also has no other reason for its existence. Attempts have been made to formulate the relationship between mission and oikoumene in such a way that
the church fulfills her apostolic task in *mission,* while in the
oikoumene she obeys the command for koinonia (communion). Koinonia is then usually viewed as the fellowship of Christian brethren. In this manner one can attempt
to make the side-by-side existence of mission and oikoumene understandable or try to legitimize it. They would
presumably supplement each other.

I believe that we would be pursuing a very dangerous
course with this kind of distinction. No matter how one
looks at it, this sort of argumentation is in the final analysis
but a refusal of the church to be nothing except an apostolic instrument. She is seeking something besides, which
is not consumed in self-denying service to the world;
something which has a "meaning" in addition to this.

The intent of the ecumenical movement could indeed be
formulated as manifestation of the Christian koinonia.
But, then, in its Biblical meaning, according to which
koinonia does not signify a static communion which one
may enjoy, but a communal and corporate participation in
Christ and his Messianic work (apostolate) in the world.[38]
Does having koinonia with others not mean that we share
with them in the proclamation of the gospel? (Phil. 1:5.)

It could perhaps be formulated a bit more sharply in
this way: In the last analysis the issue in the oikoumene is
not unity and fellowship among the churches, but a united,
corporate witness of the Kingdom to the pagan oikoumene:
unity, in order that the *world* may believe, and good works
in order that *men* may praise your Father who is in
heaven. The oikoumene, too, is nothing more than a function of the apostolate.

Now, it is of the utmost importance that we let this Messianic vision determine our actions. After all, in this lies the unity of mission and oikoumene. We will have to ask each other whether we have not become disobedient to this vision.

It is the privilege and the task of mission to prevent the oikoumene from becoming something else and being turned into a movement in which the churches are only involved with one another, so easily forgetting that the communion and the unity to which they want to give expression have meaning only when they serve the apostolate.

And it will have to be the task of the ecumenical movement to remind the missionary enterprise continually that —yes, indeed, in the heathen oikoumene!—God has already established signs of his Kingdom in the form of the young churches and that he has already spread the children of his Kingdom across the acreage of his world, in unison with whom we may let ourselves be used in a serving community for the confrontation of the world with his Kingdom.

Only when thus both movements become a function of the apostolate, can they mutually discover each other in one and the same commission (32, 154–156).

2. We are beginning to learn that the Jewish (as well as any other variety of) *proselytism* is the opposite of Christian *mission*. Usually attention is drawn only to an opposite *movement*. In the centripetal movement of proselytism, people are invited to come to the center where salvation is localized. In order to become a participant of salvation, they will have to join the group that mediates the redemption, i.e., emigrate completely from all other life relationships: in short, become a Jew. In this sphere the dominating symbol is the glory (*kabod*) of God which draws people toward itself. Mission is centrifugal. It leaves Jerusalem and the Jewish group and is on its way to the ends of the earth and the end of time. To join means here:

to join the journey away from the center. The symbol is the light for the Gentiles, which goes forth toward the people, seeking them out and taking them by surprise in their darkness.[39]

Up to this point, there is general agreement. But when a next step is in order—the radical abandonment of all that is reminiscent of proselytism in our practices—we mostly get scared and rebellious. Whole series of treatises have been written about evangelism/mission, which in the preface and the opening paragraphs give a correct exposition on the two opposite movements. But often such a correct start is followed by the wrong jump: right in the middle of church proselytism. It can be noticed in many ways, how centripetal thinking is smuggled back in; how from missionary instrument the group becomes the mediator of salvation; how baptism begins to look like a Christian ritual of circumcision, the heathen are discussed in antithetical terms in contrast to the "church" rather than in prospective terms, as those to whom the light is going out and upon whom it already shines. Finally, the church even assumes the role of Israel. It sees its primary task in terms of concentration on itself. It goes the typical Jewish way of *von aussen nach innen* (Rosenzweig) and exchanges the light of the heathen completely for the glory of which it desires to be the bearer.

It seems to me that in our further deliberations we should venture to forsake all those moralizing judgments about proselytizing (the "buying of consciences" is wrong, we don't have to discuss that anymore; and to say that one ought to be a gentleman in ecclesiastical dealings as well, is all right just for once), and begin to think through radically what exactly *mission as contrast to proselytism* means, I am convinced that the projects in which the Department on Mission Studies of the World Council of Churches is engaged (e.g., about a Biblical theology of missions) can help us a good deal here. (64, 106–107.)

III

APOSTOLATE: COMMUNICATING WITH FELLOW TRAVELERS

A. The Fourth Man

ALMOST WITHOUT EXCEPTION *the churches in Western Europe still function only in a part of the cultural milieu of the "third" man,* that product of classical and "Christian" civilization which is embodied in the European spirit with its culture of personality.[1] We still know somewhat how to handle this man, who as a type is secretly presupposed in our church work. We can associate with him, because we speak the same cultural language and share with him a respect for more or less the same values. Even when he is "unchurched" we still have so much in common with him that communication remains possible. The tradition, which has become flesh and blood in him, has never put him out of our reach. In the sociological and ideological sense he has remained a figure at the periphery of the church.

This "third man" is the stereotype address for our evangelization. Virtually all existing work is attuned to him. We presume to know how and to what he will react. Our present-day evangelism is therefore almost exclusively *Rand-Mission* (mission at the periphery). It could be called ecclesiastical coastal navigation—a spiritual engagement between neighbors.

Now, broad strata of our society have never really participated in this culture of the third man but have as a group placed themselves in opposition to it (proletariat).

In other sectors of our society, people seem to have passed
through this culture, and the third man is now appreciated
only as a somewhat curious anachronism. His position is
regarded as a viewpoint that has been overcome and that
one can ignore as long as one does not wish to be called a
reactionary. Across the line a different type of person is
advancing: the "fourth" man. Today and in the future we
will never be able to call the apostolate in these lands anything but *Rand-Mission* if we do not know how to *switch
from* the "third" to the "fourth" man.

Advent of the "Fourth" Man

The "fourth" man he has been called. Characteristically
so! He does not yet have a name, but carries a number. A
name would be the beginning of a definition. We are not
that far yet. For the time being we view him still somewhat
curiously—sometimes in the mirror—as if he is not one of
us, but only belongs in Orwell's horrible nightmare of
1984. In the meantime, he *is* here. Everywhere. But then,
the year 1984 is not so far away anymore either.

Perhaps we can sketch his profile with a bit of guessing
when we try to portray him as a *rebelling conformist*. We
need this paradox if we do not want to distort the picture
too much. Rebellion is the opposite of revolution. Revolution presupposes a historical plasticity: the belief that things
can be different and the hope that we can bring that other
day near. This faith and this hope the "fourth" man has
mainly lost. Wherever one looks, one notices an *impotence
to revolt*. One subjects oneself to the tyrant: the Fact; one
conforms completely to the "situation." Even when the
idols are recognized, they are not cast aside once and for
all, but are left standing, so that again and again they can
be slapped in the face. "The *revolutionary* wants to change
the world; he wants to project into the future, to an order
of values which he invents. . . . The *rebel* has a need to
maintain intact the abuses from which he suffers in order
to be able to rebel against them" (Sartre). In a stingingly

sharp fashion Camus has portrayed the rebelling conformist in his book *The Rebel* (1954).

Clear points of view one must not expect here. This person is no "ist," without further ado; he is not just pro or
con. He always retains a rebelling reservation. After all,
what could be accepted or rejected without qualification?

If one poses as an atheist, immediately the complaint
follows, "It's such an unfortunate thing that God doesn't
exist," and in book and play God is dragged to the stage in
order that quarrels with him can be continued. If the word
"nihilism" is mentioned, then there follows a hasty enumeration of the things that are still valued and for which one
would risk one's life. When a hymn of praise to freedom
is raised, it is not without the bitter refrain, "We are
damned to freedom." If someone praises *life,* then one can
hear, "In this life we have been thrown without any purpose or meaning." And when the longing for God can no
longer be concealed, then the complaint resounds, "Why
hast thou forsaken me?"[2]

Previous generations found their symbol in Prometheus,
the undaunted revolutionary who has dreamed up a new
future for mankind and who now is going to bring it about,
striving boldly after the divine crown. Goethe recognized
this symbol almost two hundred years ago (1773); Shelley
has glorified it romantically in his *Prometheus Unbound*
(1819) and has thus set the tone for the subsequent era
of Promethean revolutions.[3]

Our generation is in the process of exchanging this symbol for another one: Sisyphus, the "hero of absurdity," who
mockingly plods along, although he knows that the whole
business does not contain a single promise. Every attempt
to give meaning he brushes aside as treason and "spiritual
suicide." He tries to unlearn hope. Camus wrote his *Myth
of Sisyphus* in 1944.

In the meantime, this sisyphean existence is marked by
incessant boredom. We remember from one of Sartre's

books that when Antoine Roquentin suddenly discovers that he *is*, and we would expect a shock to go through his being, the only thing that follows is this dull little sentence: "I yawn long and softly." This yawning boredom lies behind so much busyness and noisy ideology. It is often as if in an opera we hear the whole chorus sing fortissimo, "We are marching! We are marching!" but nobody advances. We will not understand the bragging song if we do not notice that in the meantime everybody in boredom is marching in place; we don't understand the ideology quite right if it escapes us that it is often used merely as a hand to cover the yawning mouth. We overestimate the rebellion if we forget that it is the resistance of a conformist, who really discovered long ago that it is all so meaningless. It is the scream of a trapped animal.

This fourth man has become our traveling companion. He is *all question,* asking us to join him on this path of merciless self-exposure and secret self-justification. We cannot just classify him as a literary phenomenon of our time, as some sort of whimsical fashionist, and then place him in our cabinet for curios. From book, drama, and song he has stepped into the street and has entered our living rooms (hearts?). In the world of today we cannot take a step *without* him, nor are we allowed to turn merely *against* him; we will have to go *with* him. "When someone asks you to go one mile, go with him two miles."

However, the "fourth" man is not merely a question. He is also *an apocalyptic sign.* His advent "sign"-ifies and manifests *das Ende der Neuzeit* (the end of the modern era) (Guardini). "What now?" we ask. We don't know. Right now we can say little more than what this newest time, *our* time, is *no longer.* We live in a *post* time, just as the "fourth" man has been called a *post* phenomenon. He lives in a situation that could be characterized as *post-Christian, post-ecclesiastical, post-bourgeois, post-personal* (with, as an open question, *post-religious?*). We will now have to consider what this implies for the apostolate.

"Post-Christian"

The term is vulnerable. *After* Christ nothing new can come anymore. The Alpha is the Omega. *After* him we can no longer be *un*-Christian. We cannot get away from under the shadow of the cross. Not even if we were of the opinion, as happened recently in a youth group in Paris, that he who is hanging on the cross is called Tarzan. "Post-Christian" can in the end only mean post Christendom, and that term will have to point to the fact that we have passed through the era in which "Christendom" was apparently still a life option, something with which one knew himself to be confronted and by which one was addressed. In other words, we use this term here to describe a situation in which Christendom is no longer considered relevant for life. This, of course, does not have to mean that one does not continue to decorate one's life with Christian relics, or that, especially in the boundary situations of birth, marriage, and death, the Christian rituals are not preserved. In these moments "the flax wick still smokes" in a post-Christian society as well.[4]

Now, it is the assumption of virtually all existing work of evangelism that it takes place "within Christendom." We do not dare to say that so loudly anymore, but in practice it generally becomes apparent that at least a residue of—and consequently a certain sensitiveness for—the Christian message is still thought to be present in the hearer. Across the stream, we suspect a bridgehead of a friendly power in the dialogue-partner, and we think that we can consolidate and expand through *appeal* and *memory*—an appeal to what still lies dormant (*réveil*) (revival is still the usual form of evangelism) and a reminder of what has once been. The classic hymn of evangelism ("O Straying Sheep, Return") develops this theme of "awakening" and return and seeks to arouse memories of another past, one in which usually a devout mother "in tender youth" has played an important role.

We will have to abandon all these precious presuppositions in the apostolate outside the realm of the third man. There is nothing left that can be called into memory, nothing that can be awakened. What still might be present as "residue" is usually only some sort of forced image of a caricature Christendom. With that, one has become immune to the real thing. Every word that reminds us of this caricature will immediately be suspected. Here one must make a *new* beginning—a beginning that is not merely proclaimed but is made credible as well because it is lived in a community and is practically demonstrated in service.

All this is only to say that the apostolate in a post-Christian situation will have to lose all semblance to a "revival movement" and will have to bear the signature of *mission work*.

"Post-Ecclesiastical"

This comes out more sharply, even, when we characterize our time as post-ecclesiastical as well. Someone who returned from Russia as a prisoner of war once expressed his impressions concerning the place of the church in the West in the following image: "There is a preacher talking from behind the pulpit. We don't understand him. A glass cover has been put over the pulpit. This smothers all sound. Around the pulpit our contemporaries are standing. They too talk, and they call. But on the inside this is not understood. The glass cover smothers all sound. Thus we still *see* each other talk, but we don't understand each other anymore."

The image probably is too complimentary. It is not just a common glass cover that separates the people on the inside from those on the outside. The glass has been cut in a peculiar fashion, so that the image is distorted. From the outside they see a strange bunch of people on the inside, who have a ridiculous way of life with a curious stately dignity. A whining organ, dull singing, and a black suit are associated with "church." Christian virtues that are present

are minimized, while the kind of "church virtues" that
Dorothy Sayers once described as a combination of stateliness, childishness, shyness, dullness, sentimentality,
daintiness, and depressedness are enlarged into colossal
proportions. What would anyone want to have to do with
that?

From the inside the "outsider" too is seen in a distorted
way: a sort of hustler whom one, with a mixture of pity,
amazement, and also a little secret admiration, sees fumble
through life, all by himself.

No matter how much we vary the theme, the same motif
will always come through again: inside and outside of the
church are two worlds each seeming to conduct a mono-
logue with itself. They both talk, but they don't talk
with each other. As the fourth man sees it, the church has
so completely identified herself with the culture of the third
man that for that reason alone he will consider all that
church business as something not addressed to him. You do
not respond to it anymore with a yes or a no; you are no
longer anticlerical; you just do not have a thing to do with
it. All right, the church still *is* there, but just as there is,
for instance, a museum. He who wants to can go. But decisive decisions are not made in a museum. At the most you
pick up a few impressions there.

The attitude toward the church receives a concrete form
in the relationship toward the clergymen, who are looked
upon as "professional church people." Whether he likes it
or not, the clergyman is, in the eyes of the unchurched, the
church incarnate (he often behaves himself as if he *wants*
it that way). In the world he is treated as an outsider and
stranger, viz., one's association with him is formalized
through stereotypes.[5] There is still a place for him as
"traveling salesman in solemnities" (Germany) or, if need
be, as "the helper of the gravedigger" (France), but he can
hardly be a common friend anymore. If he wants to become that, then he will have to be dismantled and begin to
"act normally."

It seems to me that *two practical conclusions* are quite obvious in this situation. First: *the professional churchman can in general no longer be the best-suited organ for the apostolate*. His very appearance mobilizes all the post-ecclesiastical feelings and sensitivities that are present. I believe that this first conclusion is now accepted in wide circles. On this basis a drastic curtailing (among other things) of the number of full-time ministers was recently advocated.[6]

With the second conclusion, which, in my judgment, is just as obvious, we will probably face stronger opposition. *The organs of the apostolate will have to distanciate themselves as far as possible from everything that looks "churchly."* We have something else in mind than just a tactical gesture with which to meet objecting outsiders. We will have to learn to act soberly, from the realization that everything that bears a distinct "churchly" label *for that reason* already is misunderstood. Even before a word has been said, "propaganda" is suspected to be behind it, some sort of clever gimmick to gain new members for a "party," which people believe has become antiquated long ago.

We can't just *talk* away this misunderstanding; it will have to be *outlived*. Wherever in our apostolate we seek *a convincing demonstration of Christ's solidarity with the world, we* will clearly have to be present *in* this world with solidarity, not just now and then in a sortie from the ec-clesiastical enclave only to return thereafter with great, great speed, but *permanently,* because we know that as Christians we have our *Sitz im Leben* (life situation) *in the world,* not in the church. In the world one must live as a "child of the Kingdom, that has been planted on the acreage of the world."

"Post-bourgeois"

It cannot be said that we are joining those who engage in the widespread reviling ridicule of the bourgeois when we calmly state the fact that the middle-class world, as it has become expressed in the bourgeois ideology, no longer dominates our society and in any case means hardly anything to the "fourth" man.

To state this implies an admission as well that we find ourselves in the greatest perplexity. For centuries we have rendered the gospel in bourgeois categories. What is usually passed off as a "Christian" social ethics is frequently nothing but a lump of bourgeois philosophy with a Christian signature and here and there a Biblical proof text. It is difficult for us to conceive of a way to make all this plain in a different way, so that it might find a response also in a post-bourgeois situation. I believe that we have hardly ever tried it very seriously. The proclamation of the gospel in our lands has nearly always also assumed the form of *bourgeois propaganda*. Concretely, we have hardly been capable of imagining evangelism otherwise than under the dual aspect of preaching and the expansion of our bourgeois cultural atmosphere. The convert was expected to express his faith in the traditional bourgeois symbols.

This can immediately and clearly be seen from the traditional approach to the "outsiders." It was expected that he would respond as a typical middle-class man. For this reason he was thought to be reachable through *moralistic* and *apologetical* means. The preaching was continually accompanied by a strong appeal to decency and rational attitude, for moralism and rationalism were the two life elements for the bourgeois. Coupled with this went a blind confidence in words as *the* means of communication, while it was assumed—with Kierkegaard—that the "outsider" as a good citizen "dwells satisfied and securely in the realm of finiteness."

All this is more clearly brought out when we consider the pressure that is exerted on the convert to conform wholly to the *bourgeois pattern of church life*. Nonconformity is not tolerated. We find it hard to accept that outside of the bourgeois sphere an "indigenous" church could emerge, with a totally different way of doing things,

even though we remember very well that in the mission
fields a long and convincing battle has already been fought
for this. The bourgeois does not tolerate diversity and
does not understand the need for multiformity. He feels
threatened and made insecure by that which is different. He
therefore expects that the other will adjust to him. And
that in the smallest details! Not so long ago the churchly
citizen contested the right of a group of proletarian Christians to accompany their hymns with accordion rather
than organ music. That would mean an "assault on the
dignity of the gospel." And the bourgeois stands or falls
with dignity.

It seems to me that in a post-bourgeois situation the
apostolate will have to start with *a radical criticism of our
own presuppositions and forms.* For instance, we will have
to ask ourselves seriously whether it is still correct to suspect that we always have to do with a titanically self-
confident middle-class man, who must be shocked and
chased out of his false certainties. Or, whether it is still
justified to hold on to the bourgeois confidence in words
as *the* bearers of conviction now that the "fourth" man for
a long time has emptied the word into a slogan. Must we
then not seek for other means of communication? Above
all, we will have to ask ourselves whether the style of our
church life has indeed become so bourgeois that *quite
rightly* there is talk of a bourgeois ghetto where we constantly shift back and forth from apostolate to propaganda.
What will have to be changed in this church pattern to
make Christ's solidarity to the "fourth" man also more
credible?

"Post-personal"

When we come to this characterization of our time,
misunderstanding is almost inevitable. What in this connection is meant by *post-personal* is nothing more than
that the person-centered world of experience, once ac-

cepted as self-evident, has now to a large extent been exposed as fiction.

In almost every analysis of our time we meet the words *seelische Dekomposition* ("spiritual degeneration"). We experience a fragmentizing of the personality. Sometimes philosophical reflection joins in with this when the "I" is splintered or dissolved. After the "I" has become problematical as the acknowledged center, we have questioned further: "Is a real, honest relationship to 'that strange thing there' still possible? Is communication possible even with ourselves?"[7]

Thielicke has repeatedly pointed out[8] that only a small group of people dare to penetrate from their post-personal *experience* to a disciplined *reflection*. The great majority cannot exist in this thin air and flee hurriedly back into a massive traditionalism, where the "personality" continues to play a role, even though not as a fact, then yet as a myth; or it is simply accepted that the "I" is dissolved in the collective and people surrender to the world of "they."

By and large we have naïvely presupposed in our apostolate that we always have to do with people who are ready for a "personal decision." Was not all of life grouped neatly around the "I" in the evangelistic hymn, for instance, ready to be changed, if only this "I" wanted to be different! The group too was treated as an "I" in the plural; it was addressed as a gathering of personalities who were considered capable of choosing each for himself, and who were all thought to be standing on the threshold of an existential decision. If only they could hear it once more: "Choose ye this day whom you will serve!"[9]

In a post-personal situation the apostolate will have to start somewhere else. We don't really know yet where. In the confusing discussion that is presently being conducted on this matter, two ideas that will probably set the trend for the future constantly recur. We will have to work consistently in the *context of groups,* and no longer exclusively

"personal," viz., we must take into view concrete social
relationships and bring the gospel to bear within their
framework. This approach is familiar to us from the mission field. While there they frequently found themselves in
a *pre*-personal situation, where only the group can act
decisively, in our *post*-personal situation things are not
much different. Here also the apostolate must consciously
start with "group work," as, for instance, is nowadays
done among the French proletariat, where they act so
strongly from a milieu-consciousness and ever again try
to cultivate the whole *quartier* (neighborhood) as "object"
of evangelism.[10]

Many people will undoubtedly reject this *social orientation of the apostolate* with great indignation. (Who mum-
bled something already about "social gospel"?) However,
widespread sympathy will probably be found for a second
thought that frequently recurs in the present debate. In a
post-personal situation we will have to start with "a wit-
nessing *integration* of the person to the point where he
can decide." The formulation is not too fortunate, especially when in this connection there is talk of *pre*-
evangelism, which presumably must later be followed by
the "real" one. The issue is clear, however. The counseling
conversation becomes more and more a form of the
apostolate (and not merely of the pastorate). Preaching
and psychagogy are looking each other up. For our time
the center for dialogue is as typical as the mass meeting
was for a previous era.[11]

"Post-religious"?—Religion Lost

Repeatedly the "fourth" man has also been called *post-
religious*. It is claimed that in his case "the organ for the
reception of religion has been completely atrophied," that
we have to do with a new type of man—the religionless
man to whom the gospel must now be presented in a
religionless form.

Probably our definition of religion plays us a trick here. Since we don't recognize the familiar religious phenomena so easily anymore, the conclusion is drawn that the process of secularization has apparently gone so far already that even every sensitivity for a *Hintergründigkeit des Daseins* ("beyondness of existence") has been dulled. In often fantastic ways an explanation has been sought for this.[12]

I have a notion that on this point we will have to reserve our judgment for a while. Alongside of the "sober realism," we find all around us signs of a mystical, diffused religiosity. Besides the secularization, we will have to mention just as emphatically the process of a growing sacralization, which constantly makes us stand in amazement at new "transpositions and displacements of the sacred." We who operate with the categories of the "third" man can for the time being probably say no more than that for us religion has become undiscoverable and unreachable in many lives. But the "fourth" man must not be called postreligious simply because religion has been lost!

Switch Over!

"In spiritual matters the discussion is included in the therapy" (Van Nie). May we therefore, after the preceding attempt at diagnosis (even though it turned out to be so very fragmentary and so disputable), break off at this point and omit any further attempt at summarizing in a concluding paragraph what is offered us as therapy?

There are prescriptions and programs in abundance! When one studies them somewhat critically, however, it becomes apparent that most of the programs remain peculiarly vague[13] or otherwise are a mixture of commonplaces. And in the prescriptions one will in nine out of ten cases discover a proposal to restore what once existed. Sure, we say that in the apostolate we face *neu Anfange* (new beginnings) (Barth), but rarely have we been able to make that true. Let us therefore start out with the acknowledgment that we are still more or less searching, and then only in a few directions. We shrink from radical approaches, and we are mortally afraid that we will step out of line in too conspicuous a way. Even when we talk about *reformation,* we usually mean little more than the rebellion of the conformist.

Nevertheless, I think it is possible to indicate the *direction* in which many are presently seeking.

A Message of Hope

The gospel that is preached must be made understandable as *a message of hope.* It was by no means accidental that the 1954 Assembly of the World Council of Churches found its main theme in the message of hope ("The crucified Lord, the Hope of the World"), once it was decided that this Assembly as a whole should be "evangelistically oriented." Where the apostolate is taken seriously, where, in other words, we get the world clearly in view, the gospel will always become focused in a message of hope.

We feel ourselves taken up in a grand "battle for hope." In some parts of the world this is evident. There we see "Christ, our hope" confronted with and challenged by other powers in which people have put their trust with conviction. Opposed to ours we find another articulated eschatology. Therefore, in this, as in every other Promethean situation, the Christian hope will have to be proclaimed so convincingly that every other expectation is exposed as Utopia, every other hope as *false* hope.

The message of hope, however, will have to be articulated a bit differently in the West. In our situation we are rarely faced by a living eschatology, but often pass by the grave of every human expectation. In the twenty-fifth hour—the hour after the last hour—one has no knowledge of tomorrow anymore. Sisyphus is the symbol of hopelessness. Here hope will have to be learned again out of the bankruptcy of all human hope, as it is described in the works of Graham Greene. In this situation we may announce that for Christ's sake the morning will come, that we can look forward to the morning and may expect much from it. "Hope" is here the liberating but strange message, so strange, says Péguy somewhere in a moving poem, that God himself must be constantly amazed when people still can hope.[14]

To Be at Ease in the World

The message of hope—and that means hope for the world, does it not?—makes it possible again to be "worldly" in the right way. That "Christ is our hope" means that we may declare to everyone that for Christ's sake things are all right with this world, and that we may therefore move about it as free people, delivered from our cramps and filled with great expectations.

For the apostolate this opens up liberating perspectives. How miserably unworldly, how piously and puritanically we have often gone about our work. For every worldly gesture a pious excuse had to be found immediately, for every token of solidarity we had a religious purpose. We tiptoed through the world with a perennially uneasy conscience, and we behaved as if all redemptive happenings exclusively take place within the institution of the church, and as if everyone should emigrate from the world to the church in order to be saved.

Here and there we begin to discover how the message of hope also places us, who are engaged in the apostolate, in the open. We can free ourselves from all sorts of traditional fuss and bother if only we hold on to the fact that in the apostolate we are dealing with the Kingdom-for-the-world. The essence is this, that "the gospel of the Kingdom be preached in all the world," and that "the children of the Kingdom are spread across the acreage of the world." All the rest is secondary. In church and mission we are relearning all this (40, 533–565).

B. COMMUNICATION

All questions concerning the apostolate come into focus on this one point of the communication of the gospel. To speak about the communication of the gospel is not just an obvious matter, for communication is something quite different from proclamation, and it certainly encompasses much more than the classic form of proclamation: the sermon (52, 3).

Perhaps we penetrate to the core of the questions when we make a distinction between *myth* and *ideology*.

This can be illustrated from the realm of labor. In our evangelism among the laborers we have, on the one hand, the situation in which they live and, on the other hand, the ideology with which an attempt is made to explain this situation. The situation can simply be observed, and it challenges us to "social action." We discover the ideology in every conversation, for an ideology is an organized system of emotions and thoughts, through which an attempt is made to explain one's situation, and—by means of this explanation—to take hold of it.

(I suggest that ideologies are a byproduct of the industrial revolution. . . . They offer a definite plan, a blueprint for the future, a blueprint that groups may use to rationalize and to justify their revolt against the humiliating dehumanization in the secondary structure [74, 78–79].)

The ideology determines the pattern of thought and offers the rules of speech. It regulates the emotional values of everything and determines what is and what is not important. It is not a logical construction, which one could perhaps correct or follow.

Everybody has probably experienced in a discussion with a convinced Communist how easily he can abandon certain established positions. It then suddenly seems as if all that does not matter. However, when one recapitulates the conversation, he will repeat the same arguments one thought one had refuted. Arguments don't really decide anything. For that reason, I believe, it is absolutely meaningless to approach people *apologetically* in the apostolate. In that case we can —in a more or less profound exposition—tear the "-ism" of the other to shreds, but when we have won the argument, it usually appears that we have lost the man. It is even so, that through this whole apologetic discussion one has only strengthened the other in his ideology. For he will probably always keep the idea in his head that he would have won the argument if only he had been better informed. Via this sort of apology we cannot come to a communication of the gospel. In that way we constantly remain stuck in the realm of skirmishes and never reach the real field of battle.

On this level we can only place one ideology over against another. In this way our message can only be understood as an ideology with which the other does not want to have anything to do. After all, he belongs to another "club." Consequently, it is necessary and liberating to make a distinction here between ideology and myth. The myth does not interpret the situation, but defines it. What, for instance, does a labor myth mean? I believe it means merely this: that one has consciously chosen a place somewhere in the world. The myth is not much more than an attempt to say, "Here I stand in the universe over against people and groups, over against the world of the employers, over against the world of bourgeois values, and therein also probably over against the church." The myth constitutes the group which has a common past, a past which in the labor press is constantly called into remembrance. Much more important even is the fact that the group has a common future and a common expectation: the anticipated dawn of the liberation of the people. All this welds the group into a firm solidarity. Thus all of life is not only set in a Messianic glow, but that firm solidarity, which can hardly be defined, is also explained thereby.

Of course, this myth is for the most part unconsciously present. Sometimes it bursts out into a song. Usually it remains concealed. This myth can never be completely expressed. In the labor *ideology* we discover only a very small part of the labor myth, namely that part which has to do with the social-political sphere of life. The personal part of life and family life remains in the semidarkness of the unexpressed. It is there, but it is only half articulated. We cannot talk about it anymore. It has to be lived through, and that is the great question of the apostolate. If communication is going to be possible, we will first have to live ourselves into this sphere, because this is the level of life where the decisions are made and where things receive their names.

What are we after with this schematizing of the distinctions between myth and ideology? It seems to me that this differentiation can serve as a useful tool to penetrate to the essential questions of communication. Communication becomes possible only when we have not merely discovered the myth by the other person, but have made contact with it as well. Only by knowing the myth, and by making our word—our gospel word—relevant to it, can that word regain its symbolic power and evoke in the hearer the associations that the speaker had intended. Something very different is meant hereby than that we take over the terminology of the other. The question is to discover *why* this terminology is used, *why* this particular ideology can function, and *why* an explanation for what is partly experienced mythically, is sensed in it.

We have now arrived at a wholly different level than that of adjustment and accommodation. We are here on the level where genuine communion is established and therefore also communication. Here we begin to understand something of the phenomenon of the priest-laborer as a serious attempt to participate in the labor myth and thus to make communication possible again.

Our demonstration of solidarity will have to appear in this sort of living contact. This does not mean, of course, that one joins the howling wolves in the forest or that one

must identify oneself with their thoughts. But we must try
to discover the function, the significance, the task of this
ideology and to give new names to the things that are expressed in it.

In a few brief points I will attempt to summarize what
practical consequences this has:

1. The proclamation to the outside can never be a
rehash of the sermon. Structurally it is something entirely
different from a sermon.

To state this more strongly: it is an illusion to suppose
that communication of the gospel will be possible only
through the word. Of course, God can perform miracles
through a single word, and we will have to take this rever-
ently into account. What is asked of us, however, is that
we resist every temptation to engage in an exclusively or
even primarily verbal communication. Because, through
the approach of the word alone we only reinforce the resistance by the unchurched people and further foster the
bad reputation.

2. Apologetics, which moves on the level of ideology,
can virtually never serve the communication of the gospel,
because on this level the gospel will be misunderstood as
another ideology.

We do not want to imply that such apologetics has become meaningless, but rather that it can never be considered more than an unimportant part. I believe that it
would mean a liberation if, for once, this was taken very
seriously. As church people we so often have the illusion
that we are really coming to terms with a Communist or
an existentialist when once in a while a book is written
against communism and existentialism. This could prove
to be a horrible mistake.

3. In the present situation in Western Europe, communication of the gospel will have to be seen primarily as a
demonstration of our willingness to really enter into the
living situation of the other. It is simply not true that the
church—through her members—lives in the world and

is present there. In many spheres this is definitely not the case. These spheres are only addressed in a fashion and from a far-off distance. The word is shot down there, without our realizing that it is caught in the ideological shield with which people protect themselves. It does not hit the mark.

4. This demonstration cannot take place as long as the church fearfully protects its members in its own world and wants to keep them there alone. Apostolate in our situation presupposes that ecclesiastically one is willing to enter no-man's-land. This means that a great freedom is offered to really identify oneself with others, even when their ideology is rejected. This is the opposite of what here, in the Netherlands, is called the antithesis, but it cannot be otherwise. From this it follows quite obviously that the apostolate is foremost a task for lay people, or rather, for the congregation. The congregation is the bearer of the apostolate, and she will have to make the Word and thus also the apostolate credible through her existence and life, through word and deed.

Finally, I would like to review I Cor. 9:16–23 with you for a pregnant summary of these conclusions concerning the apostolate. Paul speaks there about his apostolate and he defends it. Four thoughts come to the fore in this passage.

1. Paul states very emphatically (and the church, which is built on the foundation of the apostolate and thus lives in apostolic succession, can repeat it after him) that he has been placed under *compulsion* in the apostolate. He stresses this in order to reject the idea that he is involved in it out of his own will or voluntarily. It is a curious thought: I simply *must;* I can do none else. Woe to me if I do not preach the gospel. Because it is not done voluntarily, therefore, the apostolate cannot remain without obligation.

2. Because I live under compulsion and am not engaged in this of my own volition, I am completely *free* from the people. This compulsion of the apostolate makes me totally

free, free from the people, free from traditions and old forms. This is apparently something different from what we usually call freedom. "Because I act under divine compulsion, I am free from all principalities and powers."

3. There is, however, a limit to my freedom. This limit is called *service*. Although I am free from all people, I am a servant of all. In service we also become free from our freedom, viz., in this service we acknowledge that our freedom is a freedom for the sake of others. It is a freedom which is given us in order to be used. Often we have said that this is a sort of adjustment to the situation in which we live. But in essence the matter goes much deeper. If I adjust to someone else, I myself remain out of range, at a distance. No, says Paul, this sort of adjustment is not enough; we must be servants. We must no longer view the other as an object. In our work of evangelism we have often spoken about objects for evangelization. An object is someone or something to which one wants something to happen without serving it. There is only one limit to my freedom, namely, that I use this freedom in order to serve the other.

4. Then, finally, even this freedom is surrendered. There are two reasons for this. First, in order to win or to save the others. Secondly, in order that thus I myself might partake of the gospel (I Cor. 9:23). Perhaps this is the greatest mystery of the apostolate. We can talk about it, very profoundly even, but it always ends up in this. The mystery of the divine compulsion is not a tyranny, but it is his intention that he who lives under this compulsion shall share in the gospel also. He who wins for Christ is won himself. While serving others, one is saved oneself, and while one surrenders one's freedom in that service to all, one is served unto by Christ. Perhaps this is the final thing that we can ever say about the apostolate (52, 7–10).

IV

A CHANGED CHURCH
IN A CHANGED SOCIETY

WE—AND THAT MEANS ALL OF US—find ourselves taken up in a rapid current of history, and we *know* it. We have only to look back in time for a moment, and we become keenly aware of it again. We have (often without noticing it) left behind us many of the firm buoys which only yesterday determined our course. Now we are surrounded by a new horizon, and within its circle we discover a new landscape.

However, it is not only our environment that has changed; we ourselves have become different as well. The stage has not merely been furnished with new scenes, but on the stage new actors are moving about, who frequently appear strange and unfamiliar to us.

I write about this whole complex of shifts and changes as someone who—with you—is amazed at all this, and as one who—just as you—doesn't know quite what to make of it all.

A. ECUMENICAL STUDY TOPIC

1. Our subject, "A Changed Church in a Changed Society," has been studied in various countries during the past years. The World Council of Churches, at its meeting in New Delhi (1961), instructed one of its departments to engage in a study about new forms of congregational life in a changed world. The emphasis has been put especially on the missionary task of the church. The purpose

is to discover so-called "missionary structures," i.e., forms of church life that have something to say to the outsider and that can serve to advance the gospel farther into the world.

Never has so much interest been displayed about an ecumenical study project, not only in Europe but everywhere in the world. In every corner, small and large work groups are in action. In April, 1964, representatives of these groups met one another for the first time. On that occasion a few guidelines for further study were indicated, and at these I would like to look with you. Thus we are not dealing with the private opinion of some discussion leader. Rather, we have an opportunity to think and to speak within the only context in which church people can legitimately think and speak: in ecumenical context.

I should like to make two marginal notes to this ecumenical study project:

1. We have noticed already the great interest in this work. At closer inspection the interest seems to consist of a mixture of expectation and fear. *Expectation,* because here and there and everywhere people look with great suspense toward new possibilities to make of the church once again a "church for this time" in the full sense of the term. After all, things are not going so well as far as the advance of the gospel is concerned. In many a place the missionary fire has been extinguished. Sure, we *say* that we have "a Word for the world," and sometimes we sing it, but we seem hardly capable of making this word understandable. Behind this failure of the church of Christ to do what she has been called to do in the world, one suspects an impotence or an unwillingness to come to a genuine renewal of the church.

When we casually use this big word "renewal," we usually think of little more than some new furnishings and a few revisions in the inner architectural structure—a little shifting to the left and a little modernizing to the right. It is as if we have come to a mutual agreement that renewal may never amount to a radical change: to make *different* that which exists. The hope now is that as we seek and search and think together, we might overcome the fear that keeps us from a radical change. Therefore, there is expectation that something is going to happen, something that has been called the "liberating of our liberty," so that as free persons we shall engage in something that is truly new.

There is also *fear*—because, what might not be turned up? Is it not terribly dangerous to change the buoys, especially since at the moment ecclesiastical affairs are in such a precarious and threatened condition? Might not such a new form turn out to be like the one bird in the air, for which we don't want to exchange the ten birds that we think we have firmly in our grasp? Consequently, a mixture of expectation and fear.

2. It is already quite clear that in our study it can never be our purpose to compose something like a recipe book or a set of blueprints. The idea then would be: a congregation that understands its missionary task must look exactly like this. He who is bound to recipes or blueprints can hardly be called free.

Liberty, then, is only liberated when one is taken up in the liberating acts of God. Where? In history, of course! After all, our God is not a Baal, who is fettered to a certain portion of the world and who cannot get out of the way, who has no say outside of his territory, who cannot even get there.

Our God is not a temple dweller. In the strict sense of the word he is not even a church god. He advances through time; ever again he lets the new conquer the old. He is not a God of the *status quo,* but rather the Lord of the future, King of the history of the world, and, as such, also Head of the church.

The issue at stake now is that we remain in the open sphere, which is the arena of divine acts. We must maintain the right order in our thinking and speaking about the church. That order is God—World—Church, not God—Church—World. Only in this way will things find their proper place and will we perhaps be delivered from our fright for all that is "worldly." The history that we find recounted in the Bible starts simply in a garden and ends simply in a city. There was no altar in the garden, and eventually there will not be a temple in the city. The church has been shoved in between that worldly beginning and that worldly end, partly added in order to accompany that history.

B. Profile of the Church

The preceding remarks were offered as an indication of the background. As we now approach the foreground a little and wonder how we must view this church in the arena of divine dealings, I want to think particularly of the "Messianic community." She has received her charter in that amazing passage—Phil. 2:5 ff. *Thus* it will have to be in the church, just as it has been with the Messiah. The life of that church must be imitated from the Messiah, which means living in self-emptying (cf. NEB "made himself nothing")—the life of the servant. It means to live in such a manner that the church "takes the form of men."

Those are, in my judgment, the three directional words: *self-emptying, service, solidarity with the people.* And, of course, each of these words, as well as the three of them together, points to the Servant of the Lord, as portrayed in Isaiah: the prototype of all that can be called "Messianic," the model of the Messianic congregation.

If someone asks where the church is, then we ought to be able to answer: there, where people are emptying themselves, making themselves as nothing; there, where people serve, not just a little, but in the total service which has been imitated from the Messiah-Servant and in which the cross comes into view; and there, where the solidarity with the fellowman is not merely preached but is actually demonstrated.

Thus the church must prove her legitimacy, her "real-ness," by being there for the other. She does not exist in herself and certainly not for herself either; just as the Messiah did not exist in and for himself. Nor does the church live in coexistence with the world, but (as our brethren in East Germany like to express it) in *pro-existence*—for that world. Again, not just a little, or when it is convenient! The church, too, gives her life for the other. She knows that she can be "saved" only when she is prepared to lose herself completely. When she is trying to save herself, she has already lost herself.

One has to ask oneself what this view of the church as Messianic community means in very practical terms. What, for instance, would the budget of such a congregation (self-emptying-form of a servant-solidarity with the world) look like? How is the money appropriated? How are the available people assigned? In some countries people will speak of a "mature" church only when more than 50 per-cent of the available funds and people are used and as-signed for the "others," who are outside of this church. That is already quite a bit, and one hesitates to think what the result would be if this standard really were applied. But now, from the perspective of the Messianic com-munity, would that be enough; 51 percent for the others, is that self-emptying?

C. RENEWAL AND RESTORATION

When now, from this starting point, we begin to explore a bit around us, we notice that during, and especially after, World War II we here in Western Europe devoted much attention to the question of "the world which has become different." You may be familiar with these words. They form the title of a booklet by Eberhard Müller (*Die Welt ist anders geworden*), which has been widely distributed in this part of the world in various translations. A stream of literature has been published on this theme, always again presenting this central thought: the landscape of our world has been radically changed; now the church will have to become attuned to these changed conditions. After all, what could be gained by remaining the church for yesterday?

Fortunately, it has not remained just a matter of words and slogans. During the same years all sorts of experiments emerged, e.g., training centers of various kinds, lay institutes, the evangelical academies in Germany, where a "home of encounter" between church and world has been established. Also, in virtually all countries intimate forms of congregational life (viz., house churches) have been established, as well as communities (like Taizé, etc.). For a while the outlook was quite hopeful.

However, when now, some twenty years later, we once again survey these postwar developments, we notice that in the meantime not only are we faced with a standstill, but we must even speak of a decline. More than once it has been stated that eventually the years of the 1950's will be recorded as the years of *restoration,* i.e., of return to the old prewar forms of church life. This can probably be seen most clearly by our neighbors to the east. After the war, they had so clearly squared up with a long development that it could be expected that now, freed from a load of ballast, they would dare to venture into new things. And it has indeed happened. In the past few years it has become unmistakably clear, however, that during the 1950's a retreat from the new things to the old forms of the parish system was slowly taking place.

It is generally recognized that the parish type of congregation may still have significance in our day for the "preserving" pastorate, but that, generally speaking, it is not well suited for the "outreach" and the apostolate and that it will in any case have to be supplemented with other forms of parish life. A church that wants indeed to be pro-existent—to be there for the other—can therefore never be organized exclusively in local parishes. In its place, or at least parallel with it, all sorts of other forms of church life must be developed. If the church does not do that, she will come to stand outside of her own time, and will no longer be able to serve the people who have become our contemporaries.

However, it is not necessary to look across the border. Things are hardly different in our own country. Here, too, a number of ventures had been started just in time—somewhere between 1945 and 1950—and it must be considered improbable that they would have been started thereafter. Here too we find a reaching back for the old (for instance, in the church order).

In all this the fact is usually overlooked that in that case all sorts of forms are usually recaptured, which were conceived and designed for conditions quite different from our present ones. The parish system was designed for village relationships. In the system of the city it cannot function, unless the city too is molded by a village mentality. There are, furthermore, so many memories of a past era, even though we just hold on to them. On Sunday morning we go to church about ten or eleven o'clock, because this time fell in between two feedings of the cattle. But just try to change it outside of the rural milieu!

In our whole ecclesiastical life, there is very little that would indicate that we have moved into an industrial society. Where, for instance, in our hymnbooks does one find a single reference to the factory, wages, and social justice? When do we sing about leisure time? When do all those questions come into view which occupy us so intensely from Monday through Friday? And these are only a few outward manifestations (although they speak volumes!) of the absence of the church in our time. Behind this and beneath this is by and large a strong desire to preserve all that has been. We think that we "honor our fathers and our mothers" by exact imitation.

Always again restoration is the order of the day. In the meantime we know—it can be demonstrated with the clear evidence of various investigations—that when the church in her life just orientates herself to the past, when she aims her life at "the people who are still around" (just notice how often this is said: "the people who are *still* around"), it can be predicted with certainty that her style of life will become ever more old-fashioned, more archaic, so that she becomes increasingly a foreign element in our time and finally will maintain herself only as a religious ghetto.

Sometimes we hear it whispered that we really have little to do with those "outsiders" in our "own" church life; at least, we ought not to "adjust" ourselves to them. On this point we must, I believe, learn once again what Paul writes about those "outsiders" and "unbelievers" in I Cor., ch. 14. He states there in effect that what happens inside the church ought to be understandable to the outsider who happens to walk in. No hocus-pocus in the liturgy, which can be comprehended only by the inner circle! And to a large degree this is simply a question of wanting to go "with the times." No one has the right to conceal the Christian faith in a language that cannot be understood by today's reader of the daily paper.

D. ESTRANGEMENT AND EROSION IN CHURCH LIFE

Ecclesiastical life in our part of the world finds itself at present at the point of intersection of two historical processes: The first one has been in progress for centuries and is usually referred to as the progressive *narrowing of the milieu of church life*. Usually the picture presented is one in which we see ever more and different groups becoming estranged from the church. At first there was supposed to have been the quiet exodus of the intellectuals (clearly so since the beginning of the eighteenth century). With the emergence of an industrial society the laboring people then too disappeared behind the ecclesiastical horizon. Finally, in our day, the "new middle class" is allegedly slowly becoming detached from church life, which leaves only the old middle class.

Naturally, the idea here is not that the representatives of these various milieus have left one by one (so that we would also have to win them back one by one). No, those various groups have become unchurched. Separation from the church has become something of a group pattern, a convention. When nothing happens to the milieu at large, a return of single members in substantial numbers can hardly be expected. Nowadays we prefer to see the development of the process a little differently and, I believe, much more correctly. The church has estranged herself from those milieus; *she* has withdrawn, or rather, has failed to march along as these groups established their own place in society. The church has become estranged, and consequently it is her job to "deprive" herself and to take on "the form of the fellowmen."

The second process has lasted only for a few decades. In our church life an "erosion" is taking place. The forms and, in general, the whole style have become worn and hollow. We still do the correct things, but they just don't "grip" anymore. At any rate, an explanation or commentary is needed with it, while this life in all its forms was precisely supposed to be a commentary on the faith. Thus—speaking in social terms—an ever narrower group comes to stand in the world with an ever more wornout and hollowed out style of life, which is only understandable to the few members of the inner circle. This happens in a world that long ago left this whole business behind and is all the time changing with increasing rapidity.

E. What Must We Do?

We can only indicate a few *general guidelines*. As we have already stated, we cannot present a panacea or complete blueprint.

1. *Pluralistic Church*. Usually our society is described as "pluralistic," i.e., various cultural spheres, each with

its own character, exist and interact side by side. Certainly every city dweller lives an "intersection existence" (*Schnittpunkt-existenz*). In his daily life all these various worlds cross over into one another, and in the course of a day we are called on to play a number of different roles which bear little mutual relationship to one another.

It is not easy to determine beforehand which one of those worlds is the most important. We used to believe very firmly that it was the family (house visitation!), but is this still true? Is it true across the line? Is it really still the home, or is it the place of work, or (now almost just as important) is it the sector of leisure time? That too cannot be decided beforehand once and for all. It is a fiction to presuppose in general that people really live where they reside.

In all those different worlds we relate differently to one another. In the one sphere the association involved is in intimate contact; we are engaged in regular relationships and become well acquainted. In another sphere the association is more contact-poor. We see each other, but become hardly acquainted. In another sphere again there is a fear of contact. We remain at a distance from one another and are virtual strangers.

Is it not peculiar then, that, given this situation (which, I assume, everyone knows by experience), we always again offer one model of congregational life and insist that it must be done exactly that way? Some people like to point in this connection to the "models" that have been delivered to us in Acts, chs. 2 and 4, but can we adopt these also in very different situations? Is that not possible only if similar small city relationships exist as in Jerusalem, where apparently the people lived in daily contact with one another and moved only in one sphere of life with its intimate relationships? It seems to me merciless, artificial, and simply impossible to follow this model of congregational life as *the* only one. We ourselves will have to find the forms ever anew and "in-situation." After all, the church is not our own separate society; she is not a house, but rather she qualifies the existent society as a leaven that is added to the dough.

It is understandable that in this connection many people think immediately of some outward differences, which in themselves are not so important, but which nevertheless tend to cause plenty of turmoil. For instance, should we sing in the congregation, while in our daily lives we hardly ever and hardly anywhere do that any longer en masse? Must we take cognizance of the fact that these people in their "intersection existence" also participate—let us say —in different music worlds, i.e., not only in the world of the organ and its particular atmosphere, but also in the world of jazz with its peculiar climate? However, no matter how important these questions may be, they are still only outward matters. They will automatically find a solution when we start from the assumption that a pluralistic church ought to go with a pluralistic society, a church which can be expressed in various—yes, even mutually contrasting—forms.

Of course, all this is nothing new. Seen in world context, we have answered the question concerning a pluralistic church long ago. We say of every "young church" that has developed from our missionary endeavors that "independently and in her own way, she must and may give expression to the obedience of faith." It is nonsense to behave in New Guinea as if one were in the Netherlands. We have accepted this pluralism for a long time. The question now is whether all this is allowed when we cross an ocean, but suddenly becomes prohibited when one only has to cross a street to enter into another world?

2. *Permanent Change.* We will also have to keep in mind—no matter how difficult this always proves to be— that the world has not just become different (as if all the changes are behind us, and now, for the time being we know what we are dealing with), but that, if all indications

do not deceive us, it will continue to change. The world has come into a state of *perpetual change,* and, as is being suggested from different sides, "the only thing that will remain changeless will be the constant change."

We can, therefore, not plan too much in advance. We must ever again improvise, all according to the conditions that prevail, and often without the benefit of long periods of deliberation "to look at all the angles." Perhaps a certain approach will be valid for only a few years. Groups that are being formed nowadays do not usually last longer than three to five years.

We find ourselves in an exodus-culture, and exodus will remain the order of the day. We can see it around us. How many have not left their old residences, quietly, without flying banners, almost unnoticeably and without leaving a new address behind? How many city churches have not already become pigeon-loft congregations, where people come and fly off again, and who knows where?

Where are they? In the dispersion! All of us have landed in the diaspora. The day of the big compact church blocks of hundreds or thousands of souls, who live together as neighbors, seems past. In this dispersion every church will still find "her people" here and there, in small groups. She will take the form of a diaspora-congregation.

3. *Being a Fellow Searcher.* Not only the society of which we are a part has gone afloat, thus necessitating the moving of the buoys, but we ourselves have become different as well. In our *consciousness* we have become mobile and in exodus. The word *Dauerreflektion* (Schelsky) has been used to describe a characteristic phenomenon among modern man. It refers to the attitude of being continually on the way in our thinking, always again questioning, without necessarily seeking a point of rest or a terminal point for our thinking in a definite answer. We have only to think of modern art, to sense what is at issue here.

We have become a bit weary of all those easy answers that are offered (especially in the church), often to questions that have not been raised. We do not know what to do with people who always pretend that they know it all. For this reason it is frequently so difficult for our contemporaries (and for us too) to stand it under the pulpit, from which we are often treated so childishly, as if we are not grown-up people, who can and must figure some things out for ourselves, as we are sent on the way of further questioning.

In this era of *Dauerreflektion* a catechism would have to look somewhat different from the classic kind, which gives an immediate answer to each question. It would have to lead us on a course of thinking things through with question after question after question, thus inviting us to search things out for ourselves. Whenever possible, this search should take place within the context of mutual sharing, especially in the work of lay training which will have to occupy a central position in our church life.

With reference to Jesus' temptation in the wilderness, the Russian author Dostoevsky once remarked that Jesus did not succumb to these particular satanic temptations because he refused to take recourse to power, mystery, and miracle. In the church too "must be that mind which was in Christ Jesus." Both to those within and those outside the walls of the church she must witness in powerlessness, as a fellow searcher, as "the one beggar who tells the other beggar where to find bread," without focusing on some mysterious background and without appealing to miracles, which we always think to have on our side, as supernatural proof. In short, in our witness we must be emptied from all those characteristic phenomena that can always be seen in the "propagandist."

4. *Genuine Communion.* It seems to me that this is possible only in a small group, in a community "according to the measure of human needs," where genuine personal

relationships are possible. As soon as the group becomes larger, power, mystery, and miracle will again begin to play a role.

It is perhaps one of the most remarkable ecclesiastical developments after World War II, both in Europe and America, that everywhere such small groups have emerged spontaneously: house churches, cell groups, *koinōnia* groups, etc. And not because people hope to rediscover "coziness" in such relationships (although this happens too!), but because intimate personal relationships presuppose a communion "according to the measure of man's needs." All silly stateliness and all hocus-pocus, which so often spoil our church life, can be forgotten, yes, *must* be left behind in such groups, for it just does not fit in.

Now everyone gets a chance to remove his mask and to bring up the questions that really concern him. What are those? In general, it seems to me, they are not the questions of guilt and forgiveness, which are so central in the church's proclamation. It is rather the question whether human existence is still livable. To put it quite primitively: Can one still be a Christian and at the same time be fully a modern person? And how?

Together people search for a "Torah," a way-to-life (not a law!). To give a concrete example: I know of a house church where already for years the members have sought together and traveled together on a way-to-life in the midst of an affluent society. How does one spend one's money and one's leisure time? Then the family budgets come on the table too (could that by any chance be a contemporary application of Acts 4:32 ff.?).

5. *The Calendar Question.* Also the "calendar question," so much discussed in Germany today, must be mentioned when we speak about a changed church in a changed society. The church lives according to her own annual calendar, consisting of fifty-two seven-day weeks. She did not produce it; she found it in the society in which she

was placed, and she has (with a few minor revisions) adjusted herself to this calendar, or, rather, she has synchronized her calendar with that of society.

The question now is whether this ought not to happen again, now that the calendar of an industrial society has come to look different. The annual rhythm of fifty-two weeks has been broken up by vacations; the Sunday becomes faded out in the weekend; on the day which in the past one was expected to be home, many people are now on the road.

Could all this mean that now we ought to start living according to the rhythm of this new calendar? Perhaps instead of the fifty-two Sundays, we should have ten or fifteen "Christ days" per year, festive occasions, and in between gatherings at times when people are really there? When we adamantly hold on to our ecclesiastical calendar, we easily might turn it into a religious calendar, according to which it is imposed upon people to make time for God. I thought that in the church we would want to follow an evangelical calendar through which it becomes apparent that God has time for man. What are the implications in this connection of the saying that "man has not been created for the Sabbath, but the Sabbath has been created for man"?

Here are then a few guidelines that I discern at the moment. Under each of these proposals the famous word of Bonhoeffer should be written: "We shall not know what we do not do." We will just have to go out and try.

F. ARCHITECTURE

From the previous remarks you have undoubtedly been able to draw your own conclusions about the consequences of all this with respect to *church building*. Permit me in conclusion an attempt at summarizing these consequences briefly.

In church building a shift ought to take place from *sacral architecture* to the designing of a *fellowship house*.

Not only does the church legitimize herself through her serving character, but she will want to be identified as a servant community as well. One has to be able to see it. Her liturgy consists first of all in *diakonia,* service.

The claim is frequently made that it must be evident from the architectural structure that a congregation gathers there whose members "concentrate on the redemptive mysteries." This would then mean that a sacral space must be designed, one that is separate and different from the world. This seems to me unacceptable. The redemptive mystery is not only Word and Sacrament; it is not only what takes place within the walls when the congregation gathers there. The mystery is that Christ wants to be present. According to his promise, he is not only where "two or three are gathered in his name" (Matt. 18:20), but as well in the least of his brethren, the hungry and the thirsty, the strangers and the naked, the sick and the imprisoned. (Matt. 25:31 ff.) In the New Testament the wall between liturgy and diakonia has become transparent, and both have been placed in the context of pro-existence. One must be able to notice this from our houses.

A shift *from cathedral to chapel* must take place in our church building. The cathedral is symbolic of a stable society, a permanent rest point from which Christ the King stretches his hands out in blessing to all of life, a forerunner of the last day. The chapel is the movable house, a sort of tabernacle, which in a previous era was carried along into battle. It can easily be dismantled and moved, so that it can be where the people are. This is the symbol of an era of mobility! When one dreams of church architecture in, let us say, the year 2000, one could envision—with some architects who have already previsioned this dream for us—a number of small chapels spread across the city "like telephone booths," filling stations for diaspora people. We must also be able to vacate them easily again, consequently no big investments (which is incongruous anyhow while masses of people are starving).

In our church building a shift ought to take place *from "the church at the center" to an addition to the new housing developments of our society.* In our buildings too it must become clear that the church has "no permanent city" here. She is passing through and lives as a stranger in the world. She is a *paroikia* (from which our word "parish" has been derived), a settlement outside the homeland, therefore only "added." Her house can be nothing but an addition, an annex. Perhaps one large room in a big new apartment building?

Perhaps you are beginning to wonder what all this means. May I therefore suggest that we listen in conclusion to a simple word of Pascal: "The true wellbeing of the church: when she cannot count on anything anymore but God's promise." When the Messianic community wants anything more than only that promise (for instance, certainty), then she ceases to be the congregation of the Messiah, who has promised that "the gates of hell" shall not prevail against his church. (95.)

V

THE LIFE OF THE
CHRISTIAN COMMUNITY

In every discussion on evangelism the question concerning the renewal of the church becomes acute. Otherwise, the nervous attempts at modernization that take place at the periphery of the church will always again be exposed as unreal by the stubborn conservatism in the ecclesiastical center. New "forms" remain irrelevant as long as the life of the Christian community does not witness to the fact that the old is really past. Contemporary preaching is, for the most part, neutralized by a noncontemporary structure of the church (65, 382).

Man, as he encounters us concretely in his life relationships and in the total structure of society, is our center of configuration. By taking our starting point as well as our point of orientation here, we have already relieved ourselves of a burdensome ballast of traditional concepts (26, 291).

A. The Laity

Only the laymen can really be "worldly." In everyday life they can demonstrate something of the solidarity of Christ with the world. They are the bearers of the apostolate. It will become apparent whether a church takes the apostolate seriously by the manner in which she prepares "the members of God's mission people" (that, after all, is the meaning of the word *laikoi*) for their service.

Where the layman is permitted to be only an "aid to the minister" (and then, inevitably, becomes a copy of the clergyman), where he is considered only as a more or less "active member," there he is pulled out of the world and loses his function as apostle. The result would be that our concept of the church becomes clericalized, and that from then on we can be engaged only in a somewhat peripheral mission. Where, on the other hand, everything in church life is aimed at making the layman into an articulate Christian, there it will be possible to break out of our ecclesiastical isolation and to stand once more with the gospel in the midst of the world.

In order to be able to stand clearly in the world, one should probably consciously avoid "church atmosphere," at least for the time being. It is no secret that during the past years various clergymen in different countries have discovered this, and, specifically for the sake of the apostolate, have chosen a "worldly" profession. We know what strong sympathies there are among the younger generation with the view of Simone Weil, who refused to join the church because in that case she would have to surrender her solidarity with the world. Those who entered the ecclesiastical no-man's-land were usually regarded as deserters or wishy-washy Christians. It could be, however, that here a new form of apostolate is being found, which the church must not merely tolerate, but must even encourage (42, 396–397).

A layman—a *laikos*—is a representative of God's mission people (*laos tou theou*). He constitutes the vanguard and the first thrust of the apostolate. I would venture the thesis that the minister has become unsuited for the apostolate by virtue of his ordained status. His task is a different one. He must try to equip the laity for their service (Eph. 4:12). We can see it around us: a clergyman can share in the apostolate again and do something essential in it, once he represents himself and behaves as a layman (priest-laborer). I certainly would want to reverse very decisively the usual order which has come to be accepted in our churches as the normal order: the layman is not the aid or an extension of the minister, a clergyman in miniature or (if he really tries that) in caricature, but rather, the minister is the servant of the laity. His work will have to be directed at this: that God's mission people behave as such. He himself does not appear on the stage of the world: there the layman performs. The clergyman cannot join in that—professionally he has become unsuited for it; he can do a little directing, but further especially serve as a prompter. The pulpit becomes the prompter's box. It is only too bad that the prompter can remain hidden, whereas the man in the pulpit remains so dismally visible and sometimes annoyingly present.

I thought that this was indeed the most important thing of which we ought to remind one another. Apostolate and laity belong *essentially* together. They are not two quantities which are far removed from each other, and which through all sorts of devious and clever gimmicks have to be brought together. Rather, a thinking through of the question of the apostolate leads to the conclusion that it is first and foremost the work of laymen and that the ordained ministers are only indirectly involved in it. The signs of God's shalom must, after all, be established in-the-situation. One cannot talk the shalom from the church into the world; it wants to be *lived* in the world. That must take place on the spot, precisely because shalom involves a corrective intervention, a bringing about of wholeness. Well, the layman is the figure who really lives in-the-situation. We ministers live far too much in the tradition to be able to be really and completely in-the-situation.

Let us please not misunderstand one another. I certainly do not intend to say that the layman must participate in evangelization work in his spare time, or that he must become a Sunday school superintendent. All this is excellent work in itself, but I am not thinking of the meaningful use of some leisure time. I mean to say that in one's *profession* (we almost automatically refer to it as "worldly profession," but the Reformers spoke of it as a *divine* calling) apostolate must take place. It occurs in the manner in which one is involved in one's job—dedicated, but not "praedial"—as a free man; the manner in which one is immune to the tyranny of penultimate things (professional status, money hunger) and lets oneself be captured by the ultimate things, viz., by Jesus Christ, who rules as a servant. Rarely do our words arouse amazement, but people look up when they meet a free person who uses that freedom to serve.

Perhaps you find all this a bit cheap, too much like social "do-goodism," and then immediately we come in the vicinity of a word that in our circles is meant as a scolding term, namely, "humanistic." What I am trying to say is really nothing more than what one finds written in the Sermon on the Mount, where it says, "Let your light so shine before men, that they may see your good works and give glory to your Father who is in heaven" (Matt. 5:16). It is good Reformed theology to see the glory of God, the *gloria Dei,* as the end of man and the purpose of the apostolate. That destiny and that purpose are fulfilled among people when they see the light shine. And it is stated here that they discover that light in good works.

"Good works" has often become a frightening term which causes us immediately (and quite unnecessarily) to become nervous. After all, what it simply means is that people get an insight into our lives and discover there that this life is directed at and oriented by that which is good, that it reaches out for shalom. We are not so much talking about a whole series of isolated activities, but rather about the expression of a pattern of life that speaks also when one says or does nothing. If you want this pattern of life summarized in a few words, then look at the Servant of the Lord. His life can be described in five words: election, witness, self-identification, suffering, service. Awhile ago I said that apostolate is participation in the apostleship of Jesus Christ. To this I now add that this happens by means of the acceptance, the adopting of the pattern of the life of the Servant. I would then like to render the familiar words of Phil. 2:5–11 as follows: Let this be your pattern of life, as you find it in Jesus Christ, who has emptied himself, has taken on the form of a servant, and has become like unto men.

I want to add two more brief remarks. The great danger for the layman consists in this, that in some way or another he still clericalizes himself or lets himself be clericalized. I mean that he still lets himself be maneuvered into a position in which his life becomes ecclesiasticized and he leaves the world. All right, he works there and earns his living there, but he does not dwell there anymore; rather, he seeks an escape on the safety isle in the church. That danger is certainly not imaginary. One can notice it in all sorts of small things: the layman who adopts a preacher's tone, who begins to sell unctious edifications, who beats his minister by a number of lengths in sweetness and becomes precious. In itself all this is not so tragic, but generally it betrays something of the layman's professional disease: schizophrenia. It leads to a split between the world of Sunday and the world during the rest of the week. I want to put it sharply: a clericalized layman is unsuited for the apostolate; he has become a church-domesticated layman, tamed and caged by the church—one who has betrayed his own trade and has become unfaithful to the earth.

A second question is connected with this. The clergyman and the layman—who together form God's mission people—definitely have a different function in it. Permit me to put it in this somewhat schematic way: the minister must take care of the continuity, he guards the tradition; he must preserve and may easily be a bit conservative. The layman, on the other hand, takes care of the progressive movement, thrusts himself into the actualities of life; he must develop and build.

Both these functions belong together. It is good not only when there is harmony between them but when there remains some tension as well. We must not sound the alarm when the layman can hardly stand the church any longer. That does not have to imply that he looks down upon everything as it is being done. It can also mean that the layman understands his function well and for this reason goes into loyal opposition. We are mortally afraid of those tensions and write church papers full about them, but that does not strike me as a cause for concern. Concerned we must become when the laity meekly walk in step behind the preacher. Then they have lost their function. Because then it becomes apparent that they have moved from the world into the church, and it belongs to the grandeur and misery of the layman that he experiences his membership in the church in an *extra*-ecclesiastical way (75, 114–117).

The Lord willing, a new group of Christians may emerge in the world. Shall we very hurriedly let them emigrate from the world to the established church? We have continually attempted to do this. One can adduce important reasons for it. Much more, however, is to be said against it. Because, the way the church is at present, she isolates the people from their milieu. Such conformity and identification are required that it becomes virtually impossible to be present in the world as an affirmative and free person.

It is therefore not surprising to find that almost everywhere in the apostolate, where a serious search for new ways is going on, the existence of a congregation alongside of the regular congregation is passionately defended. People have in mind a congregation which, existing beside the older one, would express the faith independently and in its own way, and would seek its own style of life. When the fear of a splitting of the church or a schism would prevent us from venturing into this experiment, we in fact bring about a break that is deadly for the apostolate, namely, the break—the schism—with the world.

Is it not possible to recognize the early Christian institution of the house church in the new congregation and to see in the house church the genuinely apostolic structure of the church in the world? (42, 397.)

B. THE HOUSE CHURCH

Everyone must have noticed that the house church members have become strikingly silent in our discussions (when they still participate in them). They know themselves surrounded, persistently followed by journalistic curiosity (the house church in the headlines?), a tourist kind of interest ("I wouldn't mind having the experience once"), and especially by a meddlesomeness, which here and there has assumed the proportions of an inquisition. One is powerless over against this sort of irrelevant interest. In such a context the mystery remains incommunicable. And this has as its result that slowly but surely the house churches move in the direction of the "hidden church," which develops alongside and over against the "official church." To the extent that the latter further institutionalizes itself and pays the price of an excessive conformism for it, the former will vanish behind the horizon as the home of the nonconformists.

Since about 1950, attention has been called to this phenomenon in various countries of Europe, but we do not really want to face it. Still we try to get hold of the whole matter in such a way that we can take a good look at it and control it. This will become increasingly less possible. Before we become too concerned about this and start acting sentimental, we will first have to survey this situation thoroughly. And, therefore, we must not let ourselves be confused by all sorts of princes of the church and preaching giants who constantly complain that they never encounter the house churches, and then conclude from this that they don't exist. They exist *elsewhere*. Well, this in the first place.

Now, secondly, everything about those house churches goes somewhat against the grain. Let it then be a one-sided exaggeration when our generation is called "the skeptic generation" or "the lonely crowd," but there is something to it. There is no universal longing for inspired relationships and it is not true that everyone wants to overcome his skeptic reservations in animated thought, if he only knew how. We have become contact-poor and contact-shy. And we hardly feel a need to change that. For many of us the "liturgical communion" of Sunday morning is too much already, and we shudder at the thought that this should now have to find a concrete extension outside the liturgy. We cry for the cathedral as "a palace for undisturbed solitude." The other person is stripped bare, even to his voice (in the pastorate by way of radio and telephone). Television sometimes seems too much already: word and image combined; we can hardly bear that. It is a known fact that frequently during the television broadcasting of a church service either the picture or the sound is turned off.

With all this we merely want to say that the house church certainly does not fit too well in our time. It does not run along the current trend, but rather counter to it. This in spite of all the conference enthusiasm. Just listen to what comes out when one wants to get down to business and, for instance, considers the forming of an apartment congregation with people in an apartment building. Horror! Everyone immediately feels threatened and put on view. All abhorrence becomes concentrated in one bewildered sentence: "But in that way one becomes a fool in the eyes of the neighbors."

Finally, when we try to understand the house church from within as that part of the hidden church to which we are almost instinctively opposed, then everything depends, in my judgment, on where we place her. This is decisive for the question of the offices, communion, and ecumenicity.

The fragmentation of the church in all sorts of small congregations is hardly a point of controversy. This is, so to speak, part of the working plan of every minister. That in practice not so much comes of it—well, that is another matter.

We do well to take our starting point with Luther, who has given a classic formulation of the principle: "Those who seriously want to be Christians and to confess the gospel in deed and word ought to write themselves in by name and perhaps *gather by themselves in a home for prayer, Scripture reading, Baptism, Holy Communion, and other Christian exercises.* In this kind of order one can know those who do not behave as Christians, punish them, reform them, cast them out or excommunicate them according to the rule of Christ (Matt.18:15 f.). Here one could also impose common aims upon the Christians, which would be contributed willingly and distributed (II Cor.9:1,2,12). One would not need a lot of grand singing there.

"Here one could also conduct Baptism and Communion in a brief and fine manner, and direct everything to the Word, prayer, and mutual love. One should have a good, brief catechism. . . . In sum, *once one has the people who seriously desire to be Christians, the orders and procedures could quickly be brought about.* However, I cannot and may not yet order or establish such a fellowship, for I do not yet have the people for it. And I do not see many who are urgently seeking it." (Preface to the German Mass.)

This is plain language. The house church is presented as a legitimate form of church life. Complete with Word and Sacrament, prayer and offering. That is to say, with all four elements which through the centuries were considered characteristic for the gathering of the congregation. The Heidelberg Catechism (Sunday 38) mentions the same four elements when it talks about the Sunday morning service of worship. We will have to maintain that *what happens on Sunday in the sanctuary can take place every-day in the house church.* With this difference, however (the plus is to be found in the house church!), that here it takes place in a context where supervision is possible, in a group where everyone knows one another and therefore can admonish one another.

Needed are *only* the people who "urgently seek it." With a little imagination and sense for style the rest can easily be arranged. Luther adds the hint that it ought not to be turned into a miniature church. Don't start a lot of singing and celebrate the Sacraments in a brief and fine way. Rather, utilize all the possibilities which exactly this kind of context offers, namely, let everything be directed toward Word, prayer, and mutual love.

It seems to me that the essential thing has thus been said. The rest is a matter of practical execution. We could leave it at this, but then we would be ducking the issues. For we find repeatedly, do we not, that the house churches are deprived of all kinds of "rights," e.g., to celebrate Holy Communion. Then we land immediately in the foolish squabble about questions of competence.

We will have to know what we are doing. This will mean, first of all, that we have to *use our freedom,* and do not need to establish or defend it. I often have the impression that our discussions on this point are nothing more than intellectual skirmishes in which we want to see all sorts of "rights" acknowledged. As soon as that has happened, we do not know very well what to do with them.

When difficulties come, we must not seek to escape them by engaging in semiclandestine affairs. When we refuse to be put off any longer with technicalities of church order and to be forced into conformism, then we will have to declare openly that we are nonconformists and act accordingly—even if, as a result, countless church and party papers are filled with loud denunciations. The church, I believe, has a crying need for a "loyal opposition," which does not get stuck in mocking sabotage, but takes a courageous stand.

But the house churches are encircled by the denomination: a church that expressly distinguishes itself from others. That is clearly a boundary line that wants to be respected. Otherwise, one must give up one's loyalty. He who lets himself be caged in by a denomination will have to respect the bars. Even if he does it, as Karl Barth has suggested, "as a captured bird, which ever again hits against the bars."

There is no other possibility for the denominational house church. Where the loyal opposition is constantly frustrated and the nonconformists are isolated and ignored, only one road remains open: the crossing of the boundaries. For many of us this is probably the only way left. And it is precisely here that the house church comes into view again, but in a different context, namely, at that place in the world where members of various denominations live and work with those who come from elsewhere and also wish to express their faith in communion with one another. There is, of course, nothing new or original in this. The great majority of mission congregations are constituted in the same way out of representatives of different churches who together form a congregation with those who, for instance, have come from heathendom or Islam. Many "categorial churches"[1] are composed in that way as well, for instance, in the armed services, in hospitals and other institutions.

It is no accident that this comparison slips into the text at this point. For it appears that in recent discussions on the "structure of the church," the mission, as well as the categorial congregation, is repeatedly portrayed as "abnormal." Here, in Western Europe, these would be admissable in only a few exceptional cases. When those cases then are sorted out (naturally, as sparingly as possible), it usually is concluded that the university students are in such an exceptional position, and therefore come into consideration as a *categorial mission church.*

Thus it is already admitted that the church in the student world cannot be modeled after the "normal" parish. She is of a different order, and it would therefore be nonsense to judge her by or compare her with the norms of the neighborhood parish.

That is quite a bit already. But it is not enough. We must not remain dependent on this judgment about our exceptional position. That is too arbitrary and too precarious. It must become clear that *the categorial mission church is a common and completely normal variety of church life*. There is nothing odd about it, and there is no need for special clauses. We must rid ourselves radically of all those parsimonious constructions.

Usually the argument runs somewhat as follows: the mission church has its place in the simple, experimental beginning stage of the church, during which obviously the maximum flexibility must be observed and a definite organization must be delayed. Broadly speaking, we have passed that stage in Europe: the church is established and consolidated; the denominational circles are closed; "normal" relationships have come into being. Except, of course, in a few areas that have remained behind—and here, among others, the students are mentioned—[2] and there a "mission situation" still prevails. Therefore, for the time being, a mission church must be permitted in this case.

This whole argument rests, in my judgment, on a misunderstanding that is related to the clerical devaluation of the term "mission situation" which takes place here. Quite obviously, a situation is meant in which the church does not yet function normally through the offices. It becomes demonstrable with the aid, for instance, of a little sociology and some ecclesiastical counting of noses: here, yes— there, no; then, yes—now, no more. It is then assumed that the situation can change in such a fashion that there does not have to be any question about mission anymore. That will lie behind us, then, in the past perfect tense.

To me, this seems a fatal mistake. The issue is, then, no longer one of proper terminology, but rather, we are faced with the question whether in that way we can still preserve the right perspective on the gospel. The gospel presents itself as a missionary message, does it not, and we do not possess it in any other way. Wherever the gospel arrives, there a "mission situation" emerges. Not just here and there, but universally! Not just now and then, but permanently!

"The mission situation of the church is not rooted in the situation of the moment, but in the gospel itself."[3] Outside the mission situation the church would lose the gospel and would degenerate into a—not so very interesting—religious club.

The church can remain in this mission situation (called forth by the gospel!) only if she consistently structures herself as a missionary congregation. That means that she divests herself of all that cannot be used for mission, no matter how venerable, "classic," or orthodox it may be. He who—to give only one example—is constantly concerned whether the authentic reformed character of the mission congregation can be preserved is preoccupied with irrelevant matters—and is boring.

The traditional pattern of community life of the parish church will have to be tested as to its missionary usefulness as well. Until only recently this topic was taboo. For some dark reason it was attempted to keep the parish church out of the discussion, because in it we were supposed to have "the shape of the primitive church" before us, and "a hollowing out of all Christian congregational life" was feared if we deviated one inch from this community form.

This is a strange trend of thought, indeed, that runs counter to all historical evidence. For can it not easily be demonstrated that the parish church is all but "original"? It emerged during the early Middle Ages and served the expansion of the church from the city into the surrounding area. The first parish functionary was probably the collector of the ecclesiastical taxes (tithes), who was immediately followed by the village evangelist.[4] Apparently in this framework the parish church was usable as a missionary structure, namely, for the conquest of the countryside. Here the structure was found in which the church could function as missionary congregation. But we have made something very different out of it. We have canonized the parish church; from an incidental pattern it became a normative model; from a historically conditioned phenomenon it became an unchangeable divine institution.

Slowly we are trying to free ourselves once again from this forced image. We do it reluctantly and hesitantly, yet as if we were afraid to lose the handrail that must give us support. This is clearly illustrated by Brouwers,[5] for instance, who argues emphatically that the parish—as miniature church—must remain our starting point and goal in pastoral work. However, he cannot close his eyes to the fact that several categories of people are in fact not reached, nor can they any longer be reached by the parish church. For those people, it is claimed, the categorial pastoral care ought to be "expanded mightily and massively."

When the particular groups who come into consideration for the forming of such *categorial congregations* are then enumerated, we end up with the following interesting litany: "they who do not have a permanent place of residence, e.g., skippers; they who temporarily reside away from the parish, e.g., students and military personnel; the delinquent or neglected youth on whom the usual pastoral care has little hold (Does the usual pastoral care still have much hold on the non-neglected youth?); persons who live under abnormal conditions, e.g., emigrants (and migrants within the boundaries of the country?); those who have become estranged from the church (a considerable percentage!); and they who work in the large companies."

Through this incomplete litany one can already vaguely discern that the parish church does not function, or functions inadequately, as missionary congregation in a mobile society. Categorial work seems necessary to reach effectively, and then to guide along, the mobile groups as well as "those who have become estranged from the church." In our ecumenical studies we are slowly coming to the same conclusions.[6] On this point a consensus is growing that can be summarized concisely as follows: *The parish church functions only in a stable society* for which it was originally intended (e.g., in the country where things have remained the same, a situation that can scarcely be found in Western Europe anymore) *and then exclusively for the "conserving,"* and not for the "outreaching," ministry. In the modern world, in which the people are becoming "mobilites,"[7] a church that wants to enter into the missionary situation in an adequate fashion will have to structure itself as a categorial mission church. Otherwise, it will degenerate into an anachronistic "remnant church," and then it is not too far removed from some sort of association for the maintenance of religious folklore.

This lengthy detour served the purpose of pulling the *student house church* out of its forced position of an exceptional case, as well as out of the parsimonious associations that are connected with it. Inquiries have shown me that somewhat the following image is associated with this term: a Bible study group, but with a somewhat "churchly" polish, a retreat atmosphere, introvert, "pious" (says one person), "timid" (says another). In this context, now, one is supposed to deliberate (everything is turned into deliberations) "how far one can go," and then, while deliberating, one gets the university chaplain into view—a phenomenon that without fail raises the famous trio of questions concerning the offices, Communion, and ecumenicity.

Is this an insinuating caricature? I thought only partly so. Without some fire all this smoke would never have developed. We are chock-full of confused sentiments and resentments, of which we will have to rid ourselves gladly before we can ever understand the student house church as just one of the many variants of categorial mission churches.

Only thus do we get the question in the right perspective. Take the question of the offices, for instance. In the mission church this issue will start off with the question concerning the laity. It cannot be otherwise; after all, mission is a layman's game. I would venture the thesis that we almost certainly find ourselves in something other than a mission church when people first of all think of a clergyman or an elder when they hear the word "office." And one might presume that the time is past when this word gets us all excited and when we suspect all sorts of Romish tricks in it. A layman (*laikos*) is a representative of God's mission people (*laos tou theou*), an official representative of the Lord's affairs.

Concerning the main issue, we can now consider that we are in basic agreement. "That rare beast, the layman, has certainly been discovered by the contemporary church."[8] However, the consensus evaporates when we begin to inquire further. And we must do that, for from many sides it is constantly suggested that the mission church (i.e., the lay community in the vanguard) is perhaps "acceptable," but then exclusively as forecourt, "a preliminary form of the church," a halfway house between the world and the church. In order to be and to remain fully the church of Jesus Christ, an additional factor is needed, and the complement that is intended here is called "the office."

No matter how one turns it, this line of thought seems unacceptable to me. Usually we distinguish between constitutive and regulative offices. In both cases it is impossible to think of a "necessary complement" to the congregation. *Constitutive* is only the office of Jesus Christ. This would then be a comprehensive designation of what Jesus as Messiah is, has done, and now still does. To say it in the words of our hymnbook: the acknowledgment that the Lord still continues in our day with his glorious work.

It goes without saying that one cannot speak in this case of a complement. This office is the prerequisite for the church. It is not added to it, but precedes it. After all, the forming of a congregation is precisely that mysterious event in which people let themselves be taken up in these continuing Messianic dealings, let themselves be served by and used by Jesus, let themselves be appointed and equipped as "laity," and then begin to join in "the constant unwearied giving of divine service to men in body, mind, and spirit."[9] They are drawn into Christ's office and are thus made into missionary church. Not partly, tentatively, and incompletely, but totally. Nothing can be added to that. Jesus in the midst of his people who are gathered in his name (Matt. 18:20) is a *complete* definition of the church. He who wants more than this ends up with less. And he who still speaks about a forecourt in this connection is thinking about the wrong temple.

Those offices to which "God has appointed some in the church" are called "regulative" (I Cor. 12:28). These are concrete tasks designed for a specific purpose and all directed toward the building up and the expansion of the church. Even when the impression is created that offices "give leadership" (e.g., Rom. 12:8; I Cor. 12:28), one will have to think more of service than of rule or a "spiritual police" (as is, for instance, suggested by the language of Art. 30 in the Belgic Confession).[10] To "lead" will then mean as much as: not to lag behind anyone when it comes to being helpful.

The word "regulative" is perhaps still saying too much. The officers are not the indispensable organizers, and even less the managers. They do not design congregational strategy—that is done by the Spirit, sovereign and overpowering—but they only assist in the decisions concerning tactics. They come to the aid when that is necessary. They are ready to furnish counsel, and they reinforce the weak points. They help in the maintenance or reestablishment of unity and take care that the peace in the church is not disturbed.

We must free ourselves from that familiar image of the ordained man who forever, as a matter of course—as if moved by a built-in mechanism—maneuvers himself to the chairman's seat and talks. When in the New Testament the total work of the offices is summed up as *diakonia*, it is simply impossible that the function of a president or speaker was meant thereby. The word points more in the direction of the work a waiter does, rendering service in an inconspicuous way. "It denotes not primarily a status (although this may be implied), but a function, the function of useful service."[11]

This service then is useful—not per se necessary. What is done in the congregation can be performed by every member. "The performance of particular tasks is in no way limited to specific individuals. Everywhere in the New Testament every member was permitted to proclaim the word, baptize, and administer the Lord's Supper."[12]

There is nothing that can be said against this. It just will not do to come rushing in suddenly with historical arguments and to claim that by now we have outgrown this "primitive church" and cannot turn the clock back. After all, the point is not the place of the church in the first century, but rather we are trying to listen to the Biblical witness that qualifies the church. In that witness, as far as I can see, it is of the *essence* that the *offices,* which we see functioning in great diversity, be *relativized as a matter of principle.* They are brought into a serving relationship to the constitutive office of Jesus Christ and the lay ministry of the congregation. It is so strongly relativized that it possibly could also be absent. "It ought not to be pictured, as if a church without a solidly established 'ministry' in the sense of Paul is still unfinished and provisionally ordered," and that it still must wait for fully developed organization, without which it is not really complete in its essential being. There is no support whatever for such an interpretation. As a matter of fact, the opposite is true. The church lives through the Spirit; it structures itself through the manifold spiritual gifts; it is "complete" in Christ, where the Spirit and love rule, and it is definitely not in need of any further church order.[13]

Is this to say now that *the offices* are *superfluous?* We could put it that way, but then we would put it in the language of those who seek the minimum of existence, want to be content with that, and apprehensively and suspiciously shrug their shoulders at every extra gift. What they consider superfluous is called *superabundant* in the terminology of the gospel. It is the extra that God cannot help but give over and above that which is necessary. Perhaps we get closest to it when we accept *the offices* as a *gracious surplus*. It is not more than the explanatory footnote at the bottom of the gospel text, which could also be integrally understood without the explication. The laity are of good understanding and as far as they are concerned, a word to the wise is sufficient. However, now that God extends his care for us to the extent that he does add this postscriptum to the text, now that according to his nature, he has been willing to give more than is necessary, now that he has provided an interpreter with the film, so that it might not miss the plot—we may let ourselves be treated with this gracious surplus. "To accept" and "to let it be done to one" are the words that are used for this.

Now a practical note. If I see things correctly, the question concerning ordination is usually raised in the house churches because of a feeling of inner uncertainty. People do not rest so securely that "this now is all." Of course, it is constantly held before us that it is only a tiny bit and that we would do better to travel the road back, back to the denomination, where we may know the church to be present in its fullness (well, a part of the church) with congregation and the offices.

We would do better to close our ears to this song. The Lord himself has promised his presence to the two or three who are gathered in his name. This presence is the "fullness" of the church; in this promise lies our certainty. He who still fears that he is shortchanged should not seek *something* more, but should seek *Him* more, and let Him change his concern into boldness and courage to pursue the way—without looking back. There is no return; the road points ahead.

Finally, as conclusion: never can the establishment of a house church—or any other form of church life—be made dependent on the functioning or nonfunctioning of the (regulative) offices. In other words, we do not need to wait for anything. (If that had happened in history, very little would have come—in my opinion—of missions.) The laity have the privilege of the initiative. They ought to use it. All actual help will be welcomed, even where it comes from people who are helpers by virtue of their calling. In sum, if one expects all initiative and eventually the leadership from the ordained clergy, one underestimates the congregation. If we would think that we can easily do without this extra assistance, we overestimate ourselves and fail to appreciate God's liberality, according to which he wants to care for his people "more than abundantly" and therefore has intended them to receive a gracious surplus.

In the foregoing discussion the question concerning the Lord's Supper has also been partly answered. In any case a decision has been made on that old question whether the house churches can or are permitted to celebrate this feast. If the Lord himself is willing to be present there, he can form his Table of Communion there as well. This is once again evidence of his constitutive office. About this we may be amazed and we may rejoice in it. For it means that somewhere the death of the Lord is proclaimed again for all the world to hear,[14] communion is established, and a sign is erected of the coming great banquet, to which already now the guests are on their way from far and wide. I would not know from where we would get the right to act prohibitively here.

But that is not all. The question concerning Holy Communion goes deeper. "Everyone should question himself how far he or his denomination has made himself lord of the Lord's Supper."[15] The denominations as well as the house churches constantly run the danger that they seek to master the Table of the Lord (I Cor. 11:20). In both cases the result is the same: one starts to celebrate behind closed doors, admittance to Communion is only for members of one's own group (closed Communion). With these closed doors and the closed Communion a closed mind will eventually follow—and then there is no mutual understanding left anymore. The denomination considers the house church with its own celebration of Communion a sect or a competing church and raises warning hands. And conversely, the house church looks down on that old church with pity, where the Lord's Supper is treated so squeamishly that it becomes necessary (as presently in the Netherlands Reformed Church) to remind the ministers of their obligation to partake.

There is only one remedy against such a take-over of that which belongs to the Lord, namely, *open* Communion. With the gospel goes an open door. It does not lock itself when the last one of "our people" has entered. God desires his house to be full (cf. Luke 14:23). His ground personnel must not prevent this, make it difficult, or sabotage it by, for instance, setting up all sorts of conditions. We turn things upside down, do we not, when first we require a consensus concerning Communion (agreement on a Communion theology) before we find it possible to enter into Communion. "Christian community is the *prius* of Christian doctrinal consensus."[16] Holy Communion wants to be done ("do this in remembrance of me") and thus learned while being practiced. Furthermore, it is improbable that an agreement will ever be reached when, theologically speaking, we continue to swim on dry land. As long as we in fact withhold the medicine of reunion from one another, we must not expect too much from ecumenical prescriptions.[17]

Open Communion then. And without conditions! "He who wills may come to him," we sing in the Salvation

Army. This is not only true of the sinner's bench, but of the Table of the Lord as well.

When thus we see the doors standing wide open, we ought not to post an inspector there who asks for the password or the shibboleth. In any case, the confession and the liturgical form cannot be used for that. Around the Table of the Lord happens indeed what many fear: the confession is relativized. That is not so strange. After all, every respectable confession asks *itself* to become relativized. The liturgical form as well becomes dimmed around the Lord's Table. It becomes exposed as "a certain outmoded means of spiritual accident insurance."[18]

Once more, a practical note. If I am not mistaken, in various house churches there is a much too spasmodic preoccupation with the question of Holy Communion. As if that is the only reality that can bring the congregation up to par. Sometimes the matter is almost turned into a prestige question which must be forced. Thereby one does not shrink back from childish exaggerations and from annoyingly defiant behavior.

First we ought to ask one another calmly whether— as a reaction against the atrophying of the Lord's Supper in some churches—we are now not inclined to hypertrophy it in the house churches. That can be done, as Paul found out. He found in Corinth a congregation with the kind of sacramentalists who had staked everything on the Lord's Supper.[19] They probably celebrated it frequently and gladly. That was all right. However, then it became the isle of safety on which to withdraw from life—very pious, but a devoutness without hands and feet, which did not make a bit of difference in daily behavior. During the Communion meal, which preceded the sacrament, there was no evidence of community. Everybody had to see to it that he got his share; the one remained hungry, the other ate his fill. Look, says Paul, if thus Communion is made into an alibi for life, you just do not understand what the body of the Lord is (I Cor. 11:29). Without the restoration of community, it becomes a mockery, no matter how correctly it may be celebrated from a liturgical point of view.

We will have to keep this eleventh chapter of I Corinthians close at hand in our house churches. It will serve as a mirror for the sacramentalists of whom there are plenty among us as well. But, more in general, we need it so that, once and for all, this question of the Lord's Supper may be delivered from all nervousness and tyranny. It appears to me that the surest road to a normalization lies in the *reinstitution of the Communion meal*. Jannasch raises the rhetorical question "Can the Lord's Supper, now turned into a cultic act, reassert itself meaningfully in the modern world of the masses, as long as we do not make an attempt to lead it back to its characteristic of a *common meal?*" He answers his own question by pointing to the many small Christian fellowships in which Holy Communion is celebrated in the context of a community meal and where now a renewal in depth of the Lord's Supper has set in.[20]

Therefore, a community meal, not as a preliminary to the open Communion, as a sort of get-acquainted cure with which we must be satisfied as long as we have not achieved intercommunion,[21] but rather a community which provides a *Sitz im Leben* for the Lord's Supper. An occasion then without solemnity or ritual ado—as earthly and natural as possible, an occasion where laughing is not out of place and the curtain does not have to come down before one can proceed to the next cultic rite. A place where (could it really be?) nobody looks up with surprise or nudges the person next to him when, without introduction or preliminaries, the cup is lifted for "the believer's toast of terrible joy."[22]

During recent years such a (primitive Christian) Communion meal has been restored in several countries and churches.[23] It has led to the experience that in this framework also the question concerning Communion is raised and answered in new and surprising ways. It is then not a matter of formulations, but of communion life, which becomes incarnated in the common things of daily life and there creates community and congregational life. It seems to me that we ought to get ready to travel the same road in our house churches as already happens here and there.

Finally, a word about ecumenicity. This is not a new theme anymore, for we were already dealing with it when we "placed" the house church, and spoke about a missionary church and open Communion.

We take over the only (more or less) "official" definition that has been given of ecumenical: "The word ECUMENICAL is properly used to describe everything that relates to the whole task of the whole church to bring the gospel to the whole world."[24] It can be summarized thus: *"to be engaged with the whole church as missionary fellowship in the whole world."* After this definition had been practically ignored, it has now in these latter days come into rather general use. Barth spoke recently about the new ecumenicity which distinguishes itself favorably from the (to him unsympathetic) old ecumenicity. This new ecumenicity is, according to him, marked by its "missionary dynamics and teleology," while in the old approach the churches were almost exclusively concerned with one another in order to attain greater unity.[25]

Whether a house church is ecumenical, therefore, does not depend—as is so often assumed—on its interdenominational composition only. There exist a frightful number of interchurch coteries that beat any denomination by many lengths for their introvert attitude. There are groups where people gape at one another and thereby boldly hang out the ecumenical flag. There is no future in that, for (with due respect to the ladies) "we are not so attractive that we can go on looking at each other forever."[26]

No, the issue is what *happens* in these interchurch groups; whether one really has the world in view, as it presents itself at our threshold, and whether this world is recognized as missionary realm—going on one's way with the gospel, whether it be down the street or across the ocean. The issue is whether one holds the doors wide open for the whole church, without selection, without discrimination, yes, with an intense pleasure in the otherness of the other.

In these matters it must become clear, in my judgment, whether a house church is ecumenical. That cannot just be read from the membership rolls. But it will be noticeable to anyone who lives in the neighborhood. A house church that really functions is so improbable and mysterious for those who come into contact with it that one scratches one's head, and at the same time it is so common and so sensible that one finally feels that one gets his feet on the ground. That worry about becoming a fool in the eyes of the neighbors was not so wrong, for here one suddenly gets a "fool for Christ's sake" in front of one's door, and if at all possible, he will even get across the threshold (61).

VI

MISSION IN THE CITY

WHEN THE FIRST STONE was laid for the modern industrial cities, the church was absent from the ceremony.
In the new city the church is a Johnny-come-lately, who
reported himself present only after this young society had
designed and tried its own polity. Thus it was learned
from experience that life can also be managed without
the church.

The English statesman Disraeli keenly perceived the
situation when among the one population he distinguished
"two nations," which stood alongside each other and
opposed to each other. On the one hand the "respectables,"
grouped around throne and altar, and on the other hand,
the "poor" (it was thought that there was every reason to
designate them immediately as the "irreligious poor"),
held together in the magic realm of the factory. When a
bishop uttered the suspicion that "the church would
probably lose the city," Disraeli at once put the matter
straight: "Don't be mistaken, my Lord, the church has
nothing to lose, for she has never had the city."

This unfortunate beginning has—up until today—determined the subsequent history. Even though the "two
nations" are no longer so sharply distinguished from each
other from the economic point of view, culturally speaking
they have continued to exist as two different worlds, each
with its own attitude toward religion and the church.

In the decisive moment the city has been forsaken by the church. Let us not turn that around and act as if the city dwellers have left the church. This is repeatedly suggested, for instance, in our evangelistic hymns ("O Straying Sheep, Return"), but also—more generally—in the whole manner in which the church called the city toward it. This call did not sound very convincing anyhow. As soon as—in the nineteenth century—one began to check with one's eyes what one heard with one's own ears, it became quite noticeable that a return was not counted on.

Just look. In the sanctuaries, built by the respectables for the respectables, there was no room. Take, for instance, Sheffield in 1820: four thousand seats for the more than sixty-five thousand inhabitants. Of these, three hundred places were free (in the aisle and up in the gallery). And the poor had to be dependent on those, for who could afford every year a sum for seat rental, which was the equivalent of about one or two weeks' wages? "Your houses belie your words."

Thank God, this is not the whole story. There have always been people (true, small groups—individuals) who knew that the basic words of the church are *not* "to call back" or "to call toward one," but rather, "to go out," "to seek," "to find." These words they have translated into their own lives. They did go out, across the threshold, although not in this case to "the ends of the earth" across the ocean, but rather across the street, from the one nation into the other.

Since 1800 the theme " the European city: mission field" recurs in a great number of variations. When eventually William Booth, on the basis of his own experiences in the slums of London and other cities, formulated a plan of action, he entitled his book *In Darkest England and the Way Out*. The title is a reference to a moving report on Africa that had appeared previously (Stanley, *In Darkest Africa*). The intention is clear. The cities here in "Christian England" are not any less "dark" than that part of the world which preferably was called the black continent. Both here and there, there is only one way out: mission!

All that time the deliberators (whom—like the poor— the church always has in her midst) counseled against mission. They talked about a temporary arrears which would definitely be made up soon. They advanced profound arguments, which were all supposed to demonstrate that there could be no question of mission in "baptized Europe." A "city mission" belongs in Tokyo or Bombay, not in Berlin or London.

The deliberators have not been able to prevent the emergence of a city mission. First in Glasgow (1826), where today they still like to speak with pride about "the world's first city mission." After that in London (1835), where the London City Mission developed into the great example that was followed elsewhere, both in England and on the continent of Europe (Hamburg, 1848; Berlin, 1858). At the first international conference (1885), thirty-nine city missions were represented. At the next gathering (1899), there were already seventy-one, from nearly all European countries.

The industrialization and urbanization started at such different times in the various countries of Europe and then developed at such a different pace that it is impossible to mark the phases of development in every case with the same dates. There remains between them a clear distinction in phases.

This distinction in phases can also be noticed in the history of the (organized) mission in the city. England, and especially Scotland, had—and still has—a lead. On the continent there were those who were familiar with the work in England. The mission people in the nineteenth century definitely lived from a more "European" orientation than we, in our highly praised "ecumenical" but actually narrowly national century, are accustomed to do. The work there was followed as an example after an interval of about twenty to fifty years. This occurred in many cases after it had already been discovered across the channel that things definitely had to be done differently.

With these developments before our eyes, it might therefore be better to forget about a division of history into periods, and instead to distinguish between a few types of city mission work.

A. First, the *home mission type.* The work is directed at the traditionally unchurched part of the city's inhabitants, those of the "second nation," "the unredeemed people." Among all the differences in approach, there is a striking similarity in development, which becomes quite apparent at three points.

1. The mission has sought a tangent plane with the city, not just a few passing points of contact, but a lasting contact in a section of life that was shared together. This tangent plane was found in what we today would call the "youth care sector," in the Sunday schools (intended for children who were deprived by society of education) and the "rescue homes" (for neglected youths).

It appeared immediately how much suspicion had to be overcome. We hear about parents who anxiously kept their children home, "because they were convinced that the children were seduced to the Sunday school in order to be sold as slaves in the colonies." It was suggested that secret agents were at work in the rescue homes, who sought to recruit "our boys and girls."

The first advanced mission posts in the city did not gain the significance that had originally been expected. For instance, the Sunday school has not become "the bridge across which the next generation will come over to us." Much more modestly, it became the beachhead from which the battles against suspicion were fought. At the same time, it served as a training center. From the ranks of the Sunday school teachers came the great majority of the workers in the city mission. Especially famous became J. H. Wichern, who (via the rescue mission) became the founder of the first city mission in Germany (Hamburg, 1848) and later became "the father of home mission," and D. L. Moody, who eventually would be called "the greatest city evangelist of the nineteenth century."

From youth work the city missions slowly gained access to virtually all sectors of society where aid had to be given. The people with whom the city did not know what to do were pushed off onto it. Aid *has* been rendered in an impressive way, but against its will the city mission received the character of a social first aid service. What was given through the diaconate was often received as poor relief (and how easily one starts figuring!) or as sticky philanthropy from above (and a real man does not take that).

Finally, hardly anything was expected of the city mission except that, like an ambulance, it would ride after the events in order to care for possible victims. Then, when the city itself began to take care of its people, this ambulance was no longer needed. The city mission was left holding the bag. It was not accepted in the places where life was being molded and where an outreach to the future was ventured. It became a peripheral thing.

2. Related to this is the fact that the churches that grew from and around the mission posts often became *peripheral churches*. They remained stuck at the edge of society, even when they gathered in the center of the city. They became the spiritual home for those people who did not themselves (housewives) or did not yet themselves (children) or did no longer themselves (the elderly) play an active role in the world of the factory. For decades in a row we hear almost everywhere the same complaint: the men are "unreachable" and as soon as the children become involved in the production process, we lose them. We cannot go where the heartbeat of this second nation is; we cannot follow the rhythm of the city, etc.

A distant echo of all this can still be heard in a story that recently came to our attention. A proud father who

was taking his son to work for the first time stopped for a
moment at the city mission. "Thanks for the education so
far," he said. "Now I'll take over, because you don't understand the factory anyhow, do you?"

3. Soon we notice here and there something like a *spiritual retreat.* In the marching orders the key words were
replaced by other ones, e.g., "advance" by "hold fast,"
"offensive" by "defensive," "solidarity with the city" by
"close association with the church." The congregations
saw themselves no longer as beachheads in the city, but as
in a real hedgehog position that had to be defended to the
last man, while a sortie was not deemed possible and they
dared no longer hope for new victories.

Repeatedly it has been pointed out with satisfaction
that "our mission workers in the city are now beginning
to be more and more accepted and put to work as congregational assistants." The old feud between church and mission appears now to be settled, but the connection took
place in the wrong direction: the church did not let herself be taken up in the missionary movement toward the
city, but, the other way around, it has coordinated the
city mission, has integrated it in its own work, and so has
enclosed it.

Because of this premature ecclesiasticizing of the city
mission it has lost its freedom of movement and its thrust.
This is being frankly admitted. All sorts of necessary activities must be omitted, "because—when organized by the
city mission—they bear a too strongly ecclesiastical
stamp."

In some aspects of the work we can follow the retreat
step by step. This is especially clear in France, where the
advanced posts in the industrial cities, the *solidarités* (solidarity with the city) were changed within thirty years into
fraternités, reception centers in the vestibule of the church.
The same spiritual retreat from the second to the first nation can be noticed elsewhere. It is no coincidence that
there is less and less talk about mission in the city and that

now the term "church evangelism" is preferred. Besides being a peripheral phenomenon from the social point of view, the city mission now also becomes a peripheral phenomenon, ecclesiastically speaking.

B. The *revival type*. A different spiritual climate, and consequently also a different approach, mark the city mission work that emerged and grew from the "Second Evangelistic Revival" (1857–1905).

This powerful movement, which eventually had the people sing about "streams of blessing" and "a sea of God's love," started almost unnoticed in a church in Hamilton (Canada). In 1857 there was a spontaneous development there of several prayer groups, who met daily to "pray down the walls of Jericho, which have been erected around the unbelief in our city." The spark jumped over to other congregations. In that same year to New York, where businessmen in particular gathered daily for prayer. Here the great breakthrough took place. This "revival of prayer" spread across the whole country. England also was touched. Here, in one wave after another, the "redemptive stream" flooded across Ulster and Scotland, across London and other cities as far as Wales, where the "glorious" revival (1904–1905) caused amazement throughout the world.

From far and wide pilgrims journeyed to Wales to "see Jesus" (Weren't they singing the hymn: "Just to be there and to look on his face . . . that will be glory, be glory for me."?). Among them was the Rev. Mr. Couvée, the founder of the Utrecht City Mission. Johan de Heer discovered the power of the gospel hymn there.

The "Second Evangelistic Revival" directed its attention preferably—and sometimes exclusively—at the (big) city. When necessary, this "method" was Biblically motivated with a reference to Paul's apostolate. Now, however, the city was not seen (as in the home mission type) as being across there somewhere, in the second nation, in another world, which—via all sorts of tangent planes—had to be "approached" carefully from the first nation, the world in which the church was established. Church and city were taken together, and *together* they came to be placed over against the Kingdom of God. Both became the address for the proclamation of the gospel of the Kingdom, and in order to be able to reach both, they sought the "empty space" ("the gap," Moody called it) between church and city, in order to be able to speak and act from it in both directions.

This "dual evangelism" we also find expressed in the bylaws of the United City Mission in Utrecht (1909). We read there, "The Association seeks in all its work the extension of God's Kingdom through the saving of souls and the spiritual nourishing of the believers." In order to get into the empty space the world of the church had to be left. They had to get out of its buildings. Everyone knew that the idea of an evangelistic meeting in a church was nonsense. The evangelists therefore invited the people to a theater or stadium, in general to the kind of buildings which later in France would be called *salles neutres* (neutral halls). Or, better yet, with their tabernacles and tents they went to look the people up where they lived and worked.

A visitor to the Exposition in Chicago (1893) tells that it was "perilous to go there. Along every access road was an evangelism tent." And (it makes one's flesh creep) "they were fishing there for people." Still in other ways the ecclesiastical world had to be left. One had to part with all sorts of precious customs and usages, unlearn the sophisticated style, forget all about denominational tags, in order really to concentrate the gospel into its simplest core. This simplification took place in the addresses, in which they soberly wanted to do business for Jesus, but above all in the hymn. The singing evangelist Sankey used children's songs as gospel hymns. At the meetings he sometimes summarized the speech in an improvising way in a song (e.g., after an address on Luke, ch. 15, "See, ninety-

nine returned. . . ."). The songs he used might not always
have been pure poetry, but a child could grasp them and
not forget them again (for instance, "What a friend we
have in Jesus"). His melodies took hold, were whistled the
next day on the street by the delivery boys with their shrill
voices. They were top tunes. It became clear how popular
Sankey was when once a clown in a circus in Dublin
permitted himself an antic on him. Indignantly the es-
teemed public struck up one of Sankey's hymns and sang
the clown right out of the ring.

In the big newspapers the movement was carefully followed. The gospel had once again become "news" to
which one could easily devote a front page. "Finally," the
reporters wrote, "the Christians have discovered *the level
of the people.*" And that was precisely the reason why a
few sophisticated papers (among which were also a part
of the church press) remained at a distance. They com-
plained about "a radical popularization of the Christian
faith" and warned against "a further simplification to the
point of childishness." *The Times* inquired whether per
chance the gospel was so much oriented toward "the poor
in spirit" that the respectable people (and they, of course,
are the rich in spirit) are now further excluded. Imagine!

"When eventually you read my obituary," said Moody,
"then don't believe a thing of it. Then, more than ever,
I will live." On one of the last days of the nineteenth century the notice was printed in the paper: Moody has continued to live. He has set the tone for a new development
in city work. Even if we are hardly aware of it, most of our
present activities have been modeled after him. And time
and time again we learn how difficult (almost impossible)
it is, now nearly sixty years later, to choose different ways.
People associate the word "evangelism" immediately with
the mass meetings à la Moody (Billy Graham!). At these
occasions we still sing almost exclusively the songs of the
Second Evangelistic Revival, and apparently we consider
that so self-evident that only a few people are eagerly long-

ing for a new evangelistic hymn. The whole approach has remained virtually unchanged, including the open air meetings, the tent mission, and especially that typical orientation toward the empty space between church and city, and the dual evangelism in two directions.

It might therefore be a good thing not only to remember gratefully what we have received in this revival, but also to ask critically whether this type of work has served its purpose. I believe that it has not. The estrangement from the gospel was underestimated. They have stared themselves blind at the tens of thousands who—for every meeting anew—streamed together. It was concluded from this that *everybody* was prepared to accept the gospel, if it were only presented to him in a "popular edition." A person only had to be helped across the threshold of his hesitation. "Do not delay; Come! Do it now," and the appeal to the memory of a "tender youth," or, better yet, a devout praying mother ("Tell mother, I have been saved. Her prayer has been heard.") served to bring this about.

In those meetings one did *not* have "a cross section of the whole population," as was often claimed (preferably with a reference to John the Baptist to whom "the whole Jewish nation" reportedly went out). In a certain sense it was a select public, consisting of peripheral members and "four-wheel Christians" (those who still come to church, but only when they are driven to it on four wheels at the time of baptism, marriage, and burial). It has been of immense importance that this group has not only been reached, but has been mobilized as well. The Second Evangelistic Revival has not recruited members, but only co-workers. The purpose of the evangelism was the enlistment of new evangelists. However, it would be a mistake to hold to the opinion that the second nation was reached as well.

This is not the wisdom of hindsight. Many evangelists knew it then already. Moody, for instance, did originally exclude the "believers" from his meetings. His word was not intended for them. Later he reversed himself and often addressed himself exclusively to the believers, for the others did not come. Just the other way around, William Booth discovered later that with his evangelism he remained stuck in the peripheral church life, and then made his decisive move toward the traditionally unchurched city. In the Salvation Army the revival piety assumes a missionary form.

In summary: The Second Evangelistic Revival has slowed down the dragging process of the "erosion of church life," the process of hollowing out and decay. It has got the gospel into the street once more and made it "public." It has moved people to serve and has thus written a new page in the history of missions (abroad). But, apart from a few exceptional cases, it has not penetrated into the mission field of the European city.

C. Would there already be a third type? I do not think so. At least, it is not clearly recognizable. We are still searching, and, I fear, much too hesitantly and cautiously. We find it difficult to give up anything of the work that a previous generation has bequeathed to us. Thus we are sitting in the midst of an ancestor worship, which is as touching as it is fruitless. At meetings we like to propound the thesis that "the secret of all strategy lies in the art to withdraw in time," and then we forget to demonstrate it in practice.

New experiments are looked upon with suspicion from behind the ecclesiastical blinds. Mission work always implies a willingness to begin anew, and in the process to take into account that God has not yet exhausted his new possibilities and most probably still has some surprises in store. We must not suspect the new, while shaking our heads, but accept it while bowing our heads. Even when it cannot be found anywhere in our book.

So we have to go on a search, selecting and trying. We can only vaguely indicate the direction in which this search will move.

1. Toward a much greater *mobility*. City people have recently been called "mobilites." This term comes from America, where annually at least 20 percent of the population moves. I do not know whether we can expect the same here. In the meantime, it is certain that the people in the European cities are "nomads." This was noticed a hundred years ago. But we have continued to serve the mobile people from our immovables. We have erected one temple instead of ten tents. And we have carefully delimited the temple area (parish quarters). The mission in the city does not tolerate such immobility. It will have to use its freedom (and not have to ask for it) in order—when necessary—to act as if there were no ecclesiastical registry.

2. Toward a much greater *diversity*. There will have to be room in our work for a diversity in approach. We have only just touched the second nation. We have carefully scratched at the edge of this world. And it is obviously an all too transparent self-deception if we always again let "the laborers who are still active" serve as the proverbial swallow, which is supposed to suggest to us that we are in the middle of summer. The primary thing that is asked of us in this respect is *presence,* to be there, serving without ulterior motives, and for the time being probably also without too many words.

In conjunction with this there is room for evangelism of the old style. If we only realize in that case that we are exclusively engaged in the sector of the peripheral church people, in a rearguard battle against the progressing erosion of church life. This type of "revival" is definitely not the one key that fits all doors. It is refreshing that during the past year contemporary forms were being found for this work, and that consequently—to mention only a few things—the tyranny of the organ is slowly being overcome, our hymns move a bit more toward the cabaret tune, and eventually there will probably be made room for the combo beside the choir. But even with all this modernization, the action radius of this work remains limited. And it will be good to take this soberly into account.

A greater diversity, therefore. We are not asked to permit something different if need be—and perhaps mockingly —but to experience the joy in the otherness of the other, and to stop that high-minded business for a change, according to which we want to mold everybody in our image and likeness.

3. Toward the discovery that mission work is *lay work*. And then not the work of the lay assistant of the minister, but that of the common man and woman who remain "common" and do not let themselves be cocooned ecclesiastically. This is nothing new. Throughout history it has become clear that mission is a layman's game. But it has to be discovered every time anew. And we must not immediately think thereby of *something to do*. The work of the layman consists first of all in this, that he *is there*, present, available, as a free person, who is insensitive to the brainwashing by time, so free that he has also become free from himself, and therefore serves.

By being there in such a way, the gospel is already expressed. Our words hardly amaze anybody anymore, but when someone meets a free person, he rubs his eyes and looks up in surprise, even though he does not realize that he is thus looking into God's showcase, which he has set up in the lives of his lay people. And, "enquire inside about that which you do not find in the window!"

4. Toward the employment of *small groups*. One of the most striking developments in the apostolate since World War II is the forming and use of the small group as an organ of mission work in the city. We see about ten or a dozen people living in the realization that they have been placed as a miniature church in the world, to serve as a center of radiation (*centre de rayonnement*). The strength of these groups lies in their sense of community. They are not a closed club where one constantly takes the other's spiritual temperature, but an open circle, inviting and re-

cruiting, among whom the "outsider" has the feeling that he is welcome. Thus there are house and apartment churches, groups in business establishments and student groups, neighborhood fellowships and "Protestant Orders," who have already gained an important role in the mission to the city.

5. Toward *cooperation*. John Wesley declared during the First Revival, "The world is my parish." In practice we use a different and improved text with a little different sequence: "My parish is the world." Of course, we know that "something" exists outside. We can even call it by name. After all, we are not illiterates. Once in a while we even do something "together." Of course, these have to be very special occasions, such as Christian festivals or times of crisis. After that we return to our own world, where we spent the feastless days and the times of "normal" needs. For "Christ is divided" (I Cor. 1:12).

Have we really got hold of the right question? It is not, "Is cooperation possible?" That would be arguing from the point of view of the church. From the point of view of the city—and do we not like to say so often that the church is here for the world?—the question goes like this "Is the mission possible at all except in unity?"

"When the first stone was laid for the modern industrial cities, the church was absent from the ceremony." Now she presents herself in fourfold, tenfold. Could it be that in that way the church has still *remained absent?* Then the mission in the city would still have to start. What do you think? (62.)

CHURCH AND RACE
(*with focus on South Africa*)

IN THE TITLE, we find the precarious word "and." This
could be taken to mean that we consider *church* and *race*
as two quantities over against each other. Not only would
this become terribly boring (for in that case everyone
would know from the start where we would come out),
but it would be confusing as well and prohibit a little
better understanding of the South African situation. It is
true that Luther stated that "even a child of seven knows
what the church is," but since that time we have unlearned
that somewhat. And what "race" means is certainly still a
mystery.

Furthermore, as soon as we start operating with such
categories, we irrevocably entrap ourselves. The concept
of race is a social myth. When we take this myth seriously,
we become its captives. We cannot get rid of it anymore.
Just read the many "liberal" or "progressive" treatises,
especially those published in church circles. In them it is
emphatically argued that across the racial barriers a new
unity is given, which must now find embodiment in our
lives. But the myth of race is traced so carefully, corrected,
perhaps ridiculed, that the whole issue gets far too much
emphasis in the argument and one is actually engaged in
reinforcing the prestige of the concept. Antidiscrimination
movements as well make society as a whole more "race"
conscious. It is therefore not surprising that, for instance,
in a recent survey of the attitude of the American churches

toward the Negro, it could be stated side by side that the churches are turning against discrimination more consciously than ever before—and proclaim this in very impressive declarations—while actually "they sanction and confirm the *status quo* in Negro-white relationships."[1] In other words, it is my judgment that we take the race *problem* only then seriously if we ignore it as much as possible as *race* problem.

Let us try to reduce the problems to their most simple form. Then is not this at issue: our attitude toward a person who clearly appears as someone who is "different." The "otherness" is not always visible at all. Sometimes it is only the name tag which has been put on him that makes him "different." Quite easily we can distinguish five different "attitudes," which later will return in some form or another when we deal with South Africa. Very briefly, we can characterize them as follows:

1. The first attitude is determined by *"ethnocentrism."*[2] Only the fellow tribesman or countryman is considered "a person." To be human in this atmosphere means to share in the redemption, and this is possible only if one worships the same ancestors, dwells in the same sacred land, and belongs to the same sacred people. He who belongs to another people is without salvation, and therefore essentially different from "us." The Dayaks, for instance, call him a dog or a monkey. He belongs to a different sphere and therefore ought to live separately from us as well. He can share in the salvation only if we admit him into our world. Of course, he will have to stay in his proper place —i.e., as a slave. With "us" the stranger can live only as a slave.

2. Essentially different is the second attitude. The stranger is regarded as a *heathen*. That means that he too is without salvation. We should really say that he is *yet* without salvation. Salvation has already been planned and prepared for him. He does not stand over against a closed tribe or people, but over against an open community—

open to him as well. From the eschatological perspective, the church and the heathen belong together. With the Messiah belong the heathen who honor him.

This promise is the decisive thing. Anything further we could say, for instance, about judgment is merely the reverse side of this. The No stands in the shadow of God's openhearted Yes. There is no question of the heathen's being in any way inferior or less than fully human. Even though the missionary text that was so popular at one time: "Tell the Gentiles that they are people" was not rendered correctly, the content is right. The church member stands on the same level with the heathen. Does he not know that God can raise children of Abraham out of stones? Seen from above, both are equal.[3]

3. In the Greek cultural sphere—and from there in the Western world—the stranger is viewed as *barbarian,* i.e., one who is not (cultured) and does not have (culture) what we are and have. For this reason he is considered inferior. Frequently the barbarians were portrayed as horrible monsters. They are a constant threat to our cultural sphere. A perpetual state of war exists between Greeks and barbarians. It can be no different. Plato says that "by nature they are each other's adversaries."

At a later stage this duality is broken through. Through "civilization" one can cross the critical border line between barbarian and Greek. By becoming a "man of reason," one becomes a Greek.[4]

4. The other is judged as a representative of another *class.* It is difficult to identify him. In general it can probably be explained thus: As soon as a certain social group feels threatened by another group and there is no longer a generally accepted code of behavior that could withstand this threat, the tendency is to withdraw within one's own groups and to develop a set of mores and prejudices that serve a dual function. On the one hand, they are a "road block," a limit for the other. On the other hand, they constitute a new "level." As soon as the others would adopt

our code, they belong with us.[5] The *horizontal* stratification is the peculiar mark of a class society. However, they ("classes") are not fixed once and for all. Classes are found only in a socially mobile society.

5. Finally, the *caste system*—not in the sense, of course, of a more or less exotic system in India, but as a social pattern which occurs virtually everywhere in the world. It is typical in that case that "we" and the "other" are rigidly separated from one another. Caste limits are *vertical* and nontransgressible. The system makes sense only if one believes that the other is, and therefore remains, really and essentially "different."

For about one hundred and fifty years caste distinction has usually been rationalized in biological terms. It is alleged that blood, skin color, hair, head index, shape of nose, etc., make the other different in a spiritual sense as well. He is a different kind of human being. The caste is made into a "race"—of course, an inferior one, one with whom one cannot associate. The great, unforgivable sin in the caste society is the "mixed" marriage, and every effort will be made—through legislation or social pressure—to prevent it from taking place.[6]

We are not dealing here with scientifically verifiable facts. As far as we know, according to the declaration of UNESCO, composed by experts in July, 1950,[7] "there is no difference in intelligence or temperament between the races, which could not be explained from the difference in cultural environment." However, that makes no difference whatsoever. In a caste society one pays no attention to facts, but believes in one's mythology.

In our consideration of the subject "church and race," these five types are constantly encountered, sometimes separately, usually in combination. The most common combination is undoubtedly the one between the stranger viewed as "heathen" and as "barbarian." The word *paganus* (the undeveloped heathen) contains both notions, and makes the other into a person who needs both church and school in order to be able to belong to us. How much of this still remains in our missionary thinking? In colonial history the various types can sometimes even be found in their pure form.[8]

In Spanish-Portuguese colonial politics, for instance, the colonized are the "heathen." Toynbee has explained the complete absence of racial discrimination in their polity as a residue of the Middle Ages.

In French colonial politics the colonized are treated as *pagani* (with a strong emphasis on the barbarian). Through civilization, of which the gospel is considered an aspect, they can progress into becoming French citizens.

In English and Dutch colonial politics in the past, one could speak of a mixture of class system and caste system, whereby the Dutch system was more class-oriented (the half-breed, for instance, could cross the border line) and the English system more caste-oriented (the half-breed remained a stranger). Finally, in the past German and present South African politics one found and finds the caste system almost in pure form.

However, more important than recognizing these types will be our ability to discover where exactly the great *tension areas* lie between the various groups. They are to be found in the immediate vicinity of the accepted limits. There the question is urgent whether the border line can be crossed, and if so, how. There the defensive group will put up the greatest resistance and act in the most doctrinaire fashion. And there the group in the offensive will mobilize all its powers to storm the borders. Most of the "liberals" (armchair progressives) and indifferents are to be found outside this border situation.

What are the borders? In one case one can cross the border only through a change of identity. To express it primitively, one must receive a new name, and thus become a new person. In that way one could possibly buy one's way into the sacred people. In other cases the borders can be more easily fixed, e.g., through confession and Baptism one joins the church, or development and education make it possible to leave the level of barbarian, or the acceptance of the mores and prejudices of the other class make someone a part of that group. Mixed marriages (if they were allowed!) would eventually free a group from its caste.

This was a long detour in order to enable us to characterize somewhat the situation in South Africa. Of course, everybody thinks immediately of the ominous word "apartheid." A current definition of this term in South Africa goes like this: "Apartheid is the only possible way to enable each group in the population to live according to its own nature and genius." Transposed into our terminology, apartheid means that one attempts to reduce all distinction, and thus also wishes to explain all social tensions in terms of frictions between "castes."

Until recently apartheid was merely a slogan with which Malan gained the victory in the election of 1948. In 1950, however, the Boer churches tried to give this slogan a content and thus developed a complete political program. A plea was made for territorial segregation of the various groups in the population, in order to enable every group to build its own life with its own culture, church, economy, etc. The Bantus would have to do this in a (yet to be created) "Bantustan."[9]

This program was developed at a mission conference! One can read in the report that the whole apartheid policy is nothing but a consistent application of a generally accepted missionary principle: the establishment of indigenous independent churches. How, it is asked, could a church be independent in a society dominated by whites, and how could it be indigenous if the people live spread out over the whole Union?

How could they come up with such a proposal? Immediately a historical argument is advanced. It seems as though history alone has become a valid argument there.

Ever since the establishment of the Boers in this area—
and we are reminded that this happened before the
Bantus, who now live there, had penetrated into this section—a territorial apartheid had continuously been advocated, viz., separate dwelling places. Even such "liberal"
missionaries in the nineteenth century as Dr. Philip and
W. Shaw saw in this the only possible solution to the pressing questions, although with the motivation that this was
the only way to protect the Bantu against the insatiable
land hunger of the Europeans.[10]

The thought of territorial apartheid is therefore not new
by any means. However, it has become much more complicated since the start of industrialization at the end of
the nineteenth century. At that time cheap labor was at-
tracted to the "white" areas. Unknown and uncounted
they streamed in, despite all controls. To advocate territorial apartheid now means practically that one would wish
to wipe out a piece of history. Those who now desire to
think "historically," as happens so frequently, will merely
want to return to the preindustrial period. That is the era
which the South Africans experience mythically and which
they want to materialize ever anew in celebrations (e.g.,
the Van Riebeeck Commemoration!). However, this cannot be called historical thinking anymore; at best it is
romantic.

Another aspect is even more complicated. Until the end
of the eighteenth century the inhabitants of the land were,
first of all, "heathen" as far as the Boers were concerned.
In other words, through Baptism they really ceased to be
"different." There is a story about a Hottentot woman
who was baptized and—as it says in a document—"in this
manner almost has become a European woman." A European later married her.

Therefore, Baptism was the critical limit. When that
border line had been crossed, it became difficult to maintain distinctions any longer. If one wanted to persist in
doing so, only one way remained open: mission, which led

to Baptism, had to be prohibited. Apparently this happened in the eighteenth century with the Moravian Martin Schmidt.[11] The result of this view was, among other things, that one could no longer bar the "other," who through Baptism had ceased to be an other, from one's own church communion.

During a relatively short period of time it was apparently quite normal to have "mixed" churches. In 1857 a Synod declared that it "is desirable (!) and Scriptural that, wherever this is possible, our members from the heathen should be accepted and incorporated into our existing congregations." It is true that the following was added: "Only where, because of the weakness (!) of some, this measure would hamper the cause of Christ among the heathen shall the congregations, which are already established or will yet be established from the heathen, enjoy their Christian privileges in a separate building." This was in 1880. Since then the "weakness" has become the rule. No longer did they see in the other the heathen who through Baptism became one of us, but rather, a strange creature.

One question remained. If must be, one could advocate territorial apartheid even in the church, but what about the hereafter? "Moody tells us that the question of what will happen to baptized slaves and Hottentots became a problem that concerned many, although the reference in the Bible to the many mansions in the Kingdom of Heaven, which allows the possibility of segregation in the hereafter, brought a little relief."[12]

Great changes took place in the nineteenth century, the so-called "liberal" period. In mission work, too, the other was at that time viewed especially as a pagan who, according to Dr. Philip, "will have to live separated from the Europeans only until he will have adjusted himself to the white civilization." Thereafter he is entitled to complete equality, and there may no longer be any question of apartheid.

It is important, it seems to me, that the heathen has nearly always been viewed as *paganus,* who also had to be civilized. Spreading of the knowledge of the gospel and civilization go hand in hand. Still today it can happen that during a visit to a Bantu home one gets a neatly framed Baptism certificate pressed into one's hand and is told, "You see, we are *civilized.*" Eventually all of society was thus divided into two blocks: on the one side heathen barbarism, on the other side "Christian civilization." This happened also in the Bantu village, where the school and church Bantus began to form an isolated group. Because they had crossed the critical limit, they were there regarded as outsiders. In the church, on the other hand, they were not fully accepted as members. The "weakness" did not permit this. Thus they were turned into borderline people, "discontent" elements, who did not receive what had been promised them. It is really no coincidence that the organized resistance against the pervasive caste system has been started by these baptized and educated Bantus, and is constantly nurtured by them.

The industrialization brought a new social grouping, the classes with their own solidarity. In the twenties it was thought that the class solidarity would cross the *caste* antithesis. However, it was too late. Repeatedly, the laborers have agitated (strikes), but the class struggle turned into a bitter caste (race) struggle. There was hardly a question of a proletarian solidarity. Quite to the contrary, the white proletarian became the most bitter opponent of his Bantu counterpart. Nowhere has the caste system been executed as consistently as in the labor movement. By law (Colour Bar Act) "civilized" labor has been reserved for the European, and thus the Bantu laborer has been confined to the subproletariat. The class became a caste. It is especially in order to eliminate this horizontal class warfare that the apartheid is proposed as a solution.

We ought not to judge this lightly. It is often claimed that such a system would be impracticable. For this reason

Malan and his government have immediately dissociated themselves from the program (not the general aims) of the Boer churches. But why? Why would a partition of India and Pakistan be technically possible and not this plan? That which, in my judgment, makes the apartheid program much more difficult is that it can be executed only if one were to start immediately with all sorts of discriminatory measures. Even if one were to grant that apartheid is a positive program in distinction from the negative program of segregation, it would still have to be maintained that apartheid in the future could be reached only along the road of segregation now. Can this aim really justify the means? Or does not hereby every attempt at social improvement today receive the stamp of senselessness? Concretely: Why build better homes in the industrial area of Johannesburg (see *Cry, the Beloved Country*) if in the near future the inhabitants will be shipped to Bantustan? Why educate the Bantu children, if in the next generation (in Bantustan) they become our competitors on the world market? Thus we could go on and on.

Apartheid is possible only if the caste system is immediately carried through in all spheres of life. The South African jurisprudence clearly betrays this tendency. Thus one reaches a structure of society that schematically can be portrayed somewhat like this:

CASTE LIMIT

		P		
	FEAR	O	RESISTANCE	
Culture, based		L		Barbarism, based
on Christianity		I		on heathendom
		C		
		E		
	Class		Class	
	Culture		Barbarism	
	Church		Heathen	

On the one side are (now already) pictured "black barbarism" and "heathendom." Those are the enemy powers. On the other side one finds "white civilization" and "Christianity." They must be defended. In between lies the caste limit, guarded by the police. In this way the police force is the advance post of the white caste (in such a dangerous position that recently the churches have written a special prayer service for them) and a threat to the other. "When a European needs help, he calls the police; when a Bantu is in need, he makes sure to get away from the police."

The attitude on the one side is *fear*. Nothing in South Africa has had such an impact on me as this feeling of deep-seated fear on the part of the Europeans. They realize that they are living on a volcano which might erupt any moment. On the other side the fundamental attitude becomes one of *resistance*. Not so much against anything in particular—against some specific measure or so—but, in a much more general and intangible way, against the whole system. Almost instinctively this resistance comes out in the so-called "criminality," which in South Africa has taken the form of a total revolution. Perhaps this kind of resistance has nowhere been portrayed more impressively than in the novel *Native Son,* by the Negro author Richard Wright.

The resistance is organized in the nationalistic movement, which has entered into a new stage since 1949, namely, that of the militant, anti-European sabotage technique. More than once the resistance has taken the form of "Communism," although, as far as I could gather from conversations, not in a very articulate way. One can find a sort of curiosity among the intellectuals that is merely nourished by the repeated designation of all resistance as "Communistic."

More important, however, than all those movements of resistance, which are really universal, is that of the "independent Bantu churches,"[13] in the past usually referred to as the Ethiopian movement. Here we find not only the oldest but probably also the most important expression of organized resistance against the caste system. It originates there, where the most vulnerable spot in the whole system is to be found: in the church.

Of course, not all (more than fourteen hundred different) "churches" can be easily put under one formula. Frequently these groups are disguised political organizations or sort of cooperatives, established in order to buy a piece of land as "church," while afterward the group is dissolved.

However, they all want to be "church," because this is the only independent structure which is still permitted. In some of those churches—those of the Zionistic type— one discovers ethnocentrism under the guise of the church. Now the white Christians are regarded as the strangers who are lost. True, at present they have a heaven on earth, but wait, at the gate of the real heaven stands a Bantu Peter who will not permit the whites to enter. (31, 253–263.)

What in the realm of the philosophy of culture is called negritude is usually designed as Ethiopianism in its ecclesiastical-theological projection. In this connection we naturally think first of the numerous Ethiopian Cushite churches in South Africa. The first one was established in 1892 after all sorts of tribal churches had developed. It constituted a protest against an excessive control by the European mission combined with the desire for a radical adaptation of the gospel to the African culture.

The movement spread like a prairie fire. Half a century later the number of these churches in South Africa alone is estimated at two thousand, varying from minutely small groups with a membership that could be counted on the fingers of two hands to powerful organizations, with tens of thousands of adherents, grouped around an impressive theocratic center ("Zion, Moria," etc.). All of them bear a more or less similar Ethiopian stamp.

Until recently we usually presumed that we were dealing with a typically South African phenomenon, which had to be understood and interpreted from the local situation. We have now changed this opinion, since it has become clear that the same movements can be found as well in places where there is no question of racial discrimination. For instance, there exist "Ethiopian" churches in Nigeria. Furthermore, there are Ethiopian phenomena in all sorts of prophetic, Messianic, and revival movements that have accompanied the African church almost since the beginning of its journey through the centuries.

It looks as if in the twentieth century Ethiopianism is becoming a continental phenomenon. Both world wars have served as rapids. The last one especially has produced peculiar Messiah figures. In the Upper Congo, De Gaulle was honored as the prophet and national liberator Ngol. Churchill's V-sign—together with the cross of Lorraine—has served as a liturgical symbol in a purely African church. And also what during these latter years have been called (with a horrible euphemism) disturbances are frequently offshoots or forerunners of Ethiopianism.

We will get on the track of the inspired "dogma" most easily when we understand the names Ethiopia and Cush wherever they occur in the Bible as designations of *all* of Africa. To start with, we then immediately arrive at Moses as a member of the family: his marriage to a Cushite woman (Num. 12:1) would supposedly be a first indication that the histories of Israel and Africa are interwoven from the very start. This is then further confirmed in the Scriptures. Three references serve as proof texts:

1. In The Psalms it is prophesied that "Ethiopia will hasten to stretch out her hands to God" (Ps. 68:31). Well, this can in the same way not be said of any other heathen people; it presupposes connection (covenant?) with Israel. Further evidence of this is that where an Ethiopian (= African) is mentioned in the Bible, he is assigned a place in the light circle of redemption.

2. Read I Kings, ch. 10, where the queen of Sheba (the legendary ancestress of the Ethiopian imperial house)

praises the God of Solomon (v. 9). This can be considered the first confession from African lips, the beginning of African "church" history.

3. As if this were not enough, there is still a passage in the New Testament that comes to reinforce the argument. The Ethiopian in Acts, ch. 8, can be baptized just like that, without any further delay (v. 37–38). Obviously, as an African he had already been prepared for redemption.

These meager data are then (here and there, once in a while) complemented and fabricated into a complete Ethiopian ideology. A peculiar concept of history emerges and it serves as a weapon against the "others" and as justification for the behavior of one's own group.

We hear, for instance, that the church in Africa had been established in the tenth century B.C. and maintains a separate "apostolic succession." This is a mighty weapon against all European illusions of superiority. After all, that proud continent is, all things considered, little more than a latecomer in the history of redemption. Only in Acts 16:9 do we receive the report of how finally Europe as well is drawn within the realm of redemptive history. Notice, it appears as a beggar, with a cry for help: "help us." Mark you—when the children of Ethiopia had more than a thousand years of church history behind them!

The conclusion is now obvious. The *old* church is to be found in Africa; in Europe we find the young churches. Classical Christianity is here. What the mission imports from there is secondhand; diluted, shrunk, and frizzled up during that barren detour through the cold, unfruitful, northern lands. Therefore, abandon all that unworthy longing for white Christianity. Don't fritter away your African right of the firstborn for such a miserable mess of European pottage. Most of the Ethiopian churches do not go beyond this point. This warding-off gesture is sufficient to give oneself plenty of room for an Africanization of church life. In this connection the tendency is to think exclusively of church leadership and liturgy. Crossing their heart, these people will assure you, sometimes quite vociferously and a little too pathetically to be credible, that there is no question of any dogmatic difference with the mission churches that they have left. It is a matter of schism; heresies don't play a role. It is simply a bowing to the now everywhere acknowledged majesty of nontheological factors. Or, to stick to the slogans, there is only the question of an experiment in a "parallel development in accordance with one's own peculiar nature."

Things are different in the case of some "Zionistic" churches. Here the *separate* apostolic tradition receives such a heavy accent that the ten centuries before Christ completely overshadow the twenty centuries after Christ. *Ressourcement* can then mean only a return to the sources of the Old Testament fathers. Moses becomes central as the prophet and national deliverer; John the Baptist closes the ranks of the church fathers. Leviticus-Deuteronomy are considered the heart of the Scriptures.

There a theocratic polity lies ready to be taken over immediately. That cannot be so difficult. After all, Israel and Africa live according to the same pattern, the same feeling toward life, the same customs (ritual of purification, polygamy, etc.), the same suspicion against foreign taints, the same longing for their own land, the same exuberant piety, which likes to manifest itself most of all as a "rejoicing before God" with music, song, and dance.

In their settlements these Zionists try to represent the Holy Land as exactly as possible, with a mountain Moria, a miniature Jordan, a Bethesda pool for the sick. Thus the authentic scenes and requisites are set ready; here too the drama of salvation can now be repeated, continued, and consummated. For this make-believe land of Canaan is infinitely more than portrayal. It intends to be an image of the original and a pre-view of the heavenly Canaan. In this place one gets one foot in heaven already.

More than once the New Testament is brushed aside as the "Bible of the whites." In the confession, Christ is still mentioned for memory's sake. But he proves to have disappeared from the much more spontaneous song. The history of the church is viewed in a strange and unintended intermezzo, somewhat in the way a minister looks back to and down upon the "dark ages" on Reformation Day. "History is an unnecessary detour for us, Africans, Children of Ethiopia, sons of Zion (and then the great word follows), for us, 'Israelites.' " The members of one of the biggest Zionistic churches have even started to wear a star of David as a badge. (66, 283–286.)

How complicated and intertwined the relationship between "churches and race" is in South Africa can probably nowhere be seen better than in the "independent churches." Here we are taken seriously with all our theories and excuses. We are kept to our word, and they hold the mirror before us. That is the way you have wanted it, so that is the way we now do it, with reversed prognostic, of course: lord today, slave tomorrow; heaven today, tomorrow locked out; etc. It has to come to something like this if we start to talk so energetically and loudly about "race," "national church," "independence," etc.

We see these churches standing at the end of our missionary theories. We do not claim that they are their logical consequences, but we do believe that we have too little protection in these theories against this kind of interpretation. No one can speak any longer about "indigenous independent churches" without paying serious attention to these "churches."

Still another movement is growing. One can hardly point it out with one's finger, because it can scarcely be identified. It is a kind of atmospheric change that is taking place in and outside the mission churches. An attempt is being made to find oneself in a spiritual order in which apartheid is accepted. All right, but then consistently! If the caste system is wanted, then we will accept it (out of necessity) and withdraw ourselves from all and everything from "the other side."

For the Bantu intellectuals this means, for instance, that they withdraw themselves from church and Christianity. To be a Christian is to be in danger of becoming a negative in the prestige scale of the Bantu in the same way as it was a positive yesterday. Bantu ministers now hear from their countrymen that they have become "traitors." Students are advised by all means to stay out of the churches. It is reported that in the church itself this movement is advancing. They stay at a distance from the "European churches." In the Cape province a "schismatic" movement developed in the "colored church." Last year a congregation split off, because they could no longer stand the "racial sect" which the Boer churches have become, and once again wanted to be truly "catholic," i.e., open to all.

For the future, what grows out of this mood will be of the greatest significance. Humanly speaking, hardly anything can be expected, except that another "Ethiopian movement" will grow out of it, in which the black apartheid is set over against the white apartheid which is pressing on. The more the "white bloc" will be identified with Christianity, the more the Bantu will be forced to abandon church and Christianity or to give it such an *interpretatio Africana* that this kind of Christianity becomes unrecognizable.

"What do you want?" asked an old and wise Bantu minister. "When Christian civilization comes to lie across the color line and therefore is no longer accessible to us, we will have to try to be Christian in our own way, do we not? And it is a tremendous temptation for us to want in everything exactly the opposite of what this so-called civilization stands for."

We have only offered a few loose notes, without pretensions. Perhaps it is clear why one cannot speak in a purely systematic fashion about "church and race." Everything is too mixed up to make this possible. The church is too much involved in the whole situation and also too much under a cloud to be able suddenly to free itself from it and set itself over against it. This may even be the most important thing that we must hear from South Africa, namely, that we are already *lost,* that we have already surrendered when we—no matter how partially— take the race dogma seriously.

Even if we would talk negatively about it, we have adjusted ourselves to it and unnoticeably we have let ourselves be caught in the ideology of the day. Then there can no longer be any question of freedom and authority. A church that speaks about "race" in any other way than as one of many social myths, which has to be unmasked together with the whole social mythology, has already robbed itself of the opportunity to witness with authority.

A second question: Can we, with the situation in South Africa before our eyes, speak any longer without qualification about "indigenous independent churches"?

A third question: In our ethics we suffer from a sort of social perfectionism or Utopianism. We try to solve the problems definitively and are in danger of forgetting in the process that which lies at hand, the common, the glass of cold water. With the "race" question too one should not be preoccupied in such a way that one wants to solve it once and for all. One has to try to do what lies at hand and to become willingly blind for the future. If the church would want to do *more,* she actually does less, because in that case she has turned herself into a political party.

Doing the things that lie at hand is more a matter of symbolics than logic. The contacts with the other happen mainly via symbols. They mock our logic. Logically, for instance, little can be said against calling someone a "native," and the like. These words, however, contain such a plus value that they immediately press the other into a certain scheme. A "native" can no longer be a "neighbor"; he is a specimen of a category. All this is of decisive importance in our whole discussion about the "race" question.

Now a last remark. When we talk about the "race" question in this way, we become aware that we no longer are talking only about South Africa or the United States. It is easy to pronounce judgments from a distance and to offer a "solution." Outside the boundary situation, this does not take much. However, as soon as we see one of the social myths operating here, trying to overpower us as well, and as soon as in talking about *there* we see our own lack of the real thing unmasked *here,* this discussion becomes an extremely painful affair. We are no longer talking about problems at a distance, but we know: *nostra res agitur.* Or, if one wishes to translate this phrase, we become aware that we sit on the sinners' bench *together with* our brothers in South Africa, and elsewhere, whom we do not understand and whose attitude we condemn at various points. (31, 263–266.)

VIII

THE DIACONATE

ORIGINALLY a word without much glamour, *Diakonia* must have meant something like "serving at tables" or "functioning as a waiter." It meant being subordinate, inconspicuous, available, ready to give a hand.

The Greeks thought that it was an inferior sort of business. The sophist in one of Plato's dialogues asks, "How can anyone ever be happy if he has to serve like that?"

Yet it is this word which we find at the heart of the gospel. The whole story of the New Testament, with its variety of close-ups, revolves around this one theme: For a change Someone has come, not to be served [that we know; we find it everywhere; that does not make any difference—it's nothing new!], but to serve (Mark 10:45). Everything that was done by the Son of Man who came, Jesus Christ, including humiliation, self-emptying, cross, and death, is summarized in eight letters: *diakonia*.

The same single word also indicates the pattern of life for all who follow Jesus. *Diakonia:* they go into service. They become available among men. They subordinate their plan of life to that of others. They are *other*-directed. Do not ask them how this takes place. They can hardly tell you. They find themselves among those in need; it has become their natural milieu. Here they discover that they cease to dominate. That ancient and all too clever game of power—to seek acknowledgment, to want to be served—

has lost its charm. They can no longer participate in it. They discover that they are being drawn into Jesus' diaconate and start participating in it.

Please, let us not turn this pattern of service into a program of action. That would be foolish and unrealistic. Then we will inescapably land in a vague utopianism, or (and this is worse) in a hot-tempered moralism, which chases people on with the lashes of its imperatives. One great horror!

No, the diaconate does not stand in the imperative, but rather in the promising, mood. No law is imposed, nor is one confronted with an (unattainable) ideal. One is promised a space for genuine living, and the prospect of a communicative relationship is held out.

The Christian life is assigned its place among people who need to be "served" (the Bible calls them the "poor" or "the least"). It cannot be lived elsewhere. Outside this concrete sphere of service it would wither and choke; it would become ordinary, just a pious self-seeking; uninteresting.

Well, it has been promised, "The poor you will always have in your midst" (Matt. 26:11). There will always be room, opportunity, a *Sitz im Leben,* for those who want to follow the deacon Jesus. Their "living" has been well cared for. And simultaneously the road is blocked to a disincarnate Christianity. There is no room for grandiloquent flights into heavenly spheres or for profound digging below the level where the common life is lived. The poor —"always in your midst"—prohibit that. They enable us to remain always in-situation. They compel us to stand solidly with both feet on the ground. After all, "the poor man is the concrete element par excellence—the original human fact—which dissolves the daydream and the spiritual utopianism." (E. Rideau.)

When a stranger in our Jerusalem would ask where in this world the church of the servant Jesus has been established, we ought to be able to reply without fail: "Of course, among the poor. Where else? Go visit them, and you will find the Christians there." Yes, the promise goes even farther: the poor—"always in your midst"—mark not only the Christian sphere of life; they represent Christ himself there as well. These travel companions have been given to us as a sacrament of his presence.

This can be read in that strange parable (Matt. 25:31 ff.) which, through the centuries, has served as the "Magna Charta" of the diaconate. Christ promises and gives himself in "the least," the naked, the sick, and the imprisoned. He continues to serve by coming near. Without "form or comeliness" he invites us to do what lies at hand. Thus he wants to be present in the sacrament of the poor, the "least of his brethren." We only really accept the gift of his presence through our acceptance of these "least ones." We remain in relationship with him only if we accept and live in the communicative relationship with the poor— obliging, and with a boundless respect for the hidden presence of the Lord.

From this perspective we get the diaconate into view. It means to live in solidarity with the neighbors who are qualified as the poor, and to improvise service in that situation.

Of course, this is considered much too primitive. That is not just a recent development now that the social services have been expanded enormously into a mighty apparatus, complete with ideology, casuistry, and technique. From the very start we did not know what to do with this prototype. The history of the diaconate can be written as the account of the ever-repeated attempt to detract from the original. It started in the primitive church, in the period that is usually designated as the "tunnel period." We see what enters it, and what comes out of it about fifty or a hundred years later; however, what has happened in the interim remains obscure.

This is what also happened to the deacon. He entered the tunnel as a waiter, only to come out as an assistant

to the bishop—a near-priest. He had been neatly clericalized. He had been removed from behind the backs of the
table guests and been placed somewhere at the head of
the table. And that is where he still sits in our churches,
as a respectable displaced person.

The intentions were no doubt good. In the meantime, the
effects were fatal. The deacon moved from the street, where
he belonged, to the altar space and the front bench, where
from then on he would only symbolize the service. The
solidarity became spiritualized, detached from the sphere
of direct physical contact. When we behold the dress of
the deacons (the dalmatic among the Catholics and the
black suits in many Protestant churches), it becomes immediately apparent that here only the depiction of an
idea is meant. In this uniform no one will recognize the
livery of people who are available, ready to do some
down-to-earth labor.

During the past years half a library has been written
concerning the question whether the deacon of the primitive church could return. That will be possible, it seems
to me, only when he becomes radically declericalized,
removes himself from the sacral space, disappears from the
front bench, and once again goes into the street.

The clericalization has, among other things, had the result that the diaconate became hollowed out into a service-
without-solidarity. It became bent toward philanthropy
and landed in the sphere of alms and charitable gestures.
Thereby the poor were no longer accepted as partners (and
certainly not as sacrament!), but they were degraded into
charitable objects.

This penny-pinching philanthropy has had its greatest
triumphs during the period immediately following the industrial revolution. Activities in abundance! The whole
nineteenth century was rustling with diaconal initiatives.
Experiments were conducted by both the left and the
right.

However, in this enormous business the poor were (on the whole) not accepted, but made into objects. It was done with a good deal of compassion and little respect. When the apparatus was fully erected and philanthropy had become the slogan of the day, the word was passed from one person to the next in France: "The church no longer loves the poor." This judgment could be taken over and affirmed in virtually all other countries.

In these two trends toward clericalization and philanthropy we see the diaconate lose its substance, because the given communicative relationship to the poor had been abandoned. After becoming displaced, the work lost its solidarity and became disoriented.

In the meantime a new development has been added, which has tended to discredit the spontaneous and improvising nature of the work. For a long time we have been spreading the story that our society has become so untransparent and complex that an amateur just cannot do a thing anymore. We call for the "expert," who has learned to assist as a profession—the human engineer. What at one time (so the argument continues) was a matter for many who qualified for the diaconate simply because of their willingness to serve has now become the profession of a few experts. A deacon in the classical sense is thus practically put out of the picture as a residue of a past era, and spontaneous service is apparently transplanted by a perfectionized service in which the idea of efficiency exerts a norm-suggestive power.

To me, this seems an ominous mistake. We do not have to argue about the great importance of expert knowledge. We grant that from the start. But we will have to dissociate ourselves resolutely from the forced image which has slowly grown, and which suggests that adequate information and reasonable technique can bring about service. We must free ourselves from the tyranny of methodology, procedure, or technique. It is essential for

Christian service that it take place without condition and therefore in complete freedom.

The condition of expertness or competence ought not to be set either. As soon as those restrictions are made, we are dealing with something different from *diakonia*. There must be complete freedom, even if perhaps things are then handled in a disorderly way and inefficiently. Without calculated inefficiency the nature of service rendered in freedom will be lost irrevocably.

I think that precisely in this lies the comfort and the promise for all who are engaged in the serving ministry. If they only remain in-situation, things happen which gain diaconal character in uncalculated, unexpected, and even unsuspected ways. They are fruits of the freedom, which are promised us and given to us in the sacrament of the poor. This is not merely a freedom from other powers and principalities. In the least of his brethren Christ comes to offer us the ultimate freedom; in the possibility of service he gives us freedom from ourselves. (82.)

IX

SAFETY LAST

A. ROCKY GROUND

IN THE YEAR that has gone by since the Third Assembly of the World Council of Churches, nothing more depressing has happened in things ecumenical than the endless talking about possible "responsible risks."

Up and down the country many useless words are being wasted on that subject. For, it has to be granted, the expression works as a slogan. It reminds us of the "Abrahamic Adventure," a phrase that was in everybody's mouth in previous times. And for that reason it probably will travel with us for some time to come.

We notice, however, that the conversation usually followed a fixed order: There was the promising beginning with the question from New Delhi coming as an introit: "Are we not constrained by the love of God to exert pressure on the limits of our own inherited traditions, recognizing the theological need of what we may call 'responsible risks.'" The gathering spontaneously answers, Amen, we feel constrained by the love of God, and the need (theological and otherwise) has been burning in our hearts for years.

Concrete suggestions follow: one a bit daring, but most of them so careful and cautious that one has to stretch one's imagination to discover any risk whatsoever—Hesitation. Long-drawn-out conversations to and fro, out of which slowly the classical litany is crystallized with all the well-known excuses and alibis. First conclusion (by the chairman, an experienced ecumenist): "Friends, we discover here anew the 'tragic' difference of level between the ecumenical ecstasy of world meetings and the sober realism with which we—all in our own place—must hoe among the grass roots. We shall always have, I fear, to bear the cross that is laid on us by the striking inconsistency between the church-in-writing and the church-in-action. But we keep the New Delhi vision before us and presently we shall . . ." (etc., etc.). Second conclusion (on the motion of a newcomer who has followed this strange ritual with horror): "We decide to call a study committee to undertake a new examination of the different confessional positions in the light of all the new factors introduced by the ecumenical situation, hoping that this committee will succeed in finding a way to break through the present impasse." And so, once again, the impressive mountains of confessional responsibility bore a ridiculously small (and probably even stillborn) mouse of ecumenical risks.

This experience, sketched here with a minimum of satirical exaggeration, is not important in itself. As an incident it could be ignored, for it is very well possible that the author of these lines simply spent the Year of Our Lord 1962 at the wrong spot on the globe; in the language of the parable: "on the rocky ground, where the seed had little soil; it sprouted quickly because it had no depths of earth, but when the sun rose [and the day broke to take decisions and do business] the young corn was scorched, and as it had no root, it withered away." It could, therefore, have been a somewhat exceptional situation.

However, anyone who tries to bring himself up to date on the Intercommunion discussion in the different parts of the world will be reminded of this parable over and over again. This incident seems to be a symptom: the rocky ground is a transconfessional and global phenomenon.

Time and time again a hopeful beginning is risked in order to break through the present impasse: sometimes in

a strong appeal to exert pressure on the limits of our inherited traditions (like the Open Letter to the Archbishops
by the thirty-two theologians in the Church of England,
1962);[1] sometimes in the draft of a full consensus on
Communion that marks all further excommunication as
an act of "bad faith" (like the famous Theses of Arnold-
shain in Germany).[2] But this seed did not have a chance
to get roots; little soil. "The seed sown on rocky ground
stands for the man who, on hearing the word, accepts it
at once with joy; but as it strikes no roots in him, he has
no staying power, and where there is trouble or persecution
on account of the Word he falls away at once." The temptation is great to see in the ecumenical movement the parable of the sower as a story about the rocky ground and
to bend theology into a piece of ecclesiastical geology. And
then we would be condemned to analyze the different earth
crusts, which have been shifting over each other in church
history, and to reconstruct the petrifying processes that
have resulted in the refractory soil on which we stand
today.

B. RECONNAISSANCE

This will be a task frankly annoying, soul-killing, and
without prospect. The ossified positions that have been
taken on the right and on the left are sufficiently known:
they have been mapped out and compared repeatedly during the last years; we have noted them without getting
warm about them. We know therefore—even if it is
brought up in each conversation as the latest and most
exciting news—that Intercommunion is situated differently
in the different sections of Christianity on the way to full
union.

For some it is placed at the utmost end, as the final
consummation of reunion, after it has been made clear that
a full agreement in doctrine, a mutually accepted ministry,
and an organic unity of church life exist, i.e., as a symbolic

expression of a well-proved spiritual fellowship in faith
and order.

Others put Intercommunion at the beginning, as the
necessary first step on the road, because Holy Communion
is to be used as a means of grace, not only for strengthening
the faith of the individual Christian (all confessions agree
on that) but also as a health measure for the body of
Christ; one could say, as a means of "church salvation,"
as a means of unity meant "more and more to coalesce
with Christ and so with each other" (Calvin), and therefore as a means that has to be *used* immediately because
"unity can never be reached so long as separated churches
refuse to give one another the divine medicine for their
healing."[3] Holy Communion must be celebrated together
now, proleptically and with anticipation while we are still
divided, as a mediating sign of unity (*signum unitatis*)
and an ever-tightening bond of love (*vinculum caritatis*).

A third group rejects this sterile dilemma, "starting point
or final goal," and wants to see the Sacrament as basically
"a ration for those who are on the way, of which the Lord
of the church commands that it shall be eaten with all the
saints" (II Cor. 13:12; Phil. 4:22); whatever the stage
reached in interchurch contacts, Communion *always* breaks
open the doors of the church, and it creates an ecumenical
context by itself.[4]

These are the familiar standpoints, many variations of
which naturally exist.

But this kind of information certainly does not do the
job! We are still in the middle of a somewhat vague history
of ideas (*Ideengeschichte*); in the atmosphere of disincarnate "truths"; close to abstractions. Going thus, we
shall never enter the history of the church. For the church
does not move along the inside track of profound or high-
faluting thoughts but simply remains on the surface of the
things of the day. It constitutes itself in deeds, decisions,
events. It is fully a history of realities (*Realgeschichte*),

and it wants to be that, without having to make excuses
and divested of all idealistic illusions; without respect for
religious makeup or other masquerades; with a feeling for
reality which nips in the bud all longing for "absolutistic
action" and which, without being ashamed, is satisfied
with "contextual action."[5] with always new and always
provisional improvisations. Timeless "principles" are finished; laws can be broken open by situations; the tyranny
of the paragraphs is driven out; in the history of the church,
"rules" and "exceptions" have the same dignity. How
whimsical and inconsequent reality can be is hardly demonstrated more clearly anywhere than in the *practices* of
Intercommunion. Decisions *in concreto* are taken here repeatedly, which cannot possibly be justified in principle.
Or perhaps nothing is decided at all and it simply happens.
In any case we do notice over and over again that forms
and formulas do not any longer correspond with one
another.

A few examples. Churches that emphatically proclaim
in their confession that it is sufficient (*satis*) for the restoration of churchly unity "to preach the gospel in concord
and to administer the sacrament according to the Word of
God" often appear in practice to shun Intercommunion
even when the conditions are amply fulfilled. So has it
been impossible to have a full inter-Lutheran Intercommunion,[6] even if in some parts of the world a Lutheran-
Reformed consensus on Communion could be reached.[7]
(E.g., the Netherlands, 1959.)

Groups that in principle advocate an open Communion
because they know that the *Lord's* Supper cannot be mo-
nopolized by any denomination fearfully close the door
behind them when as a minority they are confronted with
a much larger and stronger church. The whole defense
mechanism of a minority group comes into operation, and
in fact the *conception* of Holy Communion is invalidated.
But neither can we make this a general rule (i.e., a minority
position leads to closed Communion), because we see at

the same time that in a clear diaspora situation a fellowship in the Sacraments sometimes originates spontaneously—against the general expectation and also against the clear rules—when members of one church have become dispersed among other churches.

The strangest thing, however, is the "bookkeeping by double entry" that many denominations use in their Communion practice: strict and closed in the "normal" relations; free and open in relations looked upon as "abnormal." Two sets of principles: when things are normal there are rules, when things are abnormal there are exceptions (which may be canonically validated).

It is interesting to analyze where the limits lie that have to be trespassed in order to enter into "abnormal relations."

C. ABNORMALIZATION OF THE NORMAL

Well now, we are thought to pass this critical limit (1) when we get into a truly "missionary situation"; (2) when we get into an "emergency situation" that was not foreseen and therefore could not be regulated beforehand; and (3) when we have passed the point of no return in our lives and have arrived on the threshold of death.

In these three cases the possibility usually is kept open to modify and adapt generally recognized and otherwise immutable rules of church order; in these cases also Intercommunion has its best chance, even if this is otherwise excluded. When we look a bit more closely, we discover that in all three cases a situation that ought to be normal for the Christian church is abnormalized in our thinking; the normal and the daily are mentally put in the corner of the extraordinary.

1. We indeed have accepted repeatedly as proper the relaxation of strict rules on what once was called the mission field. And this has also happened in regard to Communion practice. Of course, we had our explanations and excuses for such things. Usually it was suggested that

at the first confrontation with the gospel no clear understanding could be expected for the many subtle distinctions
that are the product of a long process of inner ecclesiastical
and theological sophistication. For that reason it could be
seen as "pastorally responsible" to make a (sometimes
radical) modification of church order. However, this could
be done only in a tentative way and in exceptional cases,
because, and to the extent that, one had to deal with a
missionary situation.

It was silently understood that later—in another stage
and under more "mature" conditions—the relevance of
the traditional differences would be understood. The initial
unity, manifested for the sake of the salvation of the nations, had to be broken into denominational divisions; the
discrepancy between the exceptions in the missionary situation and the rules kept in the well-established and "historic" (whatever that may mean) churches would thus
disappear by itself.

As long as the mission field was located far away, this
meaningless rationalization was perhaps not so clearly
seen. Remarkable differences in cultural background and
life situation could make it plausible that a very flexible
and varying application of the rules was necessary. But
it becomes totally different once we in Europe, for example,
understand ever more clearly that we are placed in a true
missionary situation in our own continent. It is not necessary anymore to cross an ocean; it now suffices to cross
a street in order to enter the domain of the permitted exceptions. The confusion is terrific. In the same city and
sometimes by the same boards it is decided with the same
pathos to travel together in "a missionary situation," e.g.,
of the university community or the pastoral care of soldiers,
Intercommunion included, while at the same time (sometimes in the same church buildings!) the denominational
apartheid at the Lord's Table is defended tooth and nail.
Secretly—and sometimes quite openly—it is then hoped
that the extraordinary missionary stage will not take too

long and that before long everybody can be caged again in his strict framework of church order.

Something must have gone basically wrong in our thinking here. This probably came about because we interfered arbitrarily and began to put asunder what God had joined. He gave the gospel and got it underway in the original cluster: all nations—gospel—end of the times. Where the gospel comes, missionary situations originate, everywhere and always. It is impossible to designate *a part* as "missionary" somewhere in space or somewhere in time, which apparently can be distinguished (according to any criteria available) from the other "nonmissionary" parts: for instance, a geographically limited or sociologically determined area, which could only lie somewhere else, or a determined "history of missions," which we may leave to the past. One who wants to speak authentically about a "missionary" situation has to know that he speaks about the whole world and the whole of history, qualified as they both are by the cross and resurrection of Jesus Christ. In other words, he speaks about the normal setting of the Christian church. That which cannot serve as "order of missions" has no right to exist as order of the church. Or to say the same thing positively, what seems to be possible or admissible *extra muros,* for the sake of the salvation of the nations, will have to be legitimately possible *intra muros,* if it is not to become refined tactics. This much is self-evident: mission does not start at the walls of the church, somewhere on the periphery, but it has its source in the very heart of the church: there, where the gospel again and again constitutes an apostolic body anew. What is often admitted as an exception to the rule in a missionary situation (and then often only demurely and with all kinds of ulterior thoughts) should be valid as the normal and acknowledged rule of church order.

No bookkeeping with a double entry for, on the one hand, the church in the middle of the nations and, on the other hand, the church as a spectrum of denominations.

A bookkeeping with a single entry suffices, and such a bookkeeping is kept where the church is under way from nation to nation until the ends of the earth. And certainly, there where the means are envisaged that are intended to serve to secure the end of a full recovery and more credible manifestation of the unity of the church. For: "the true context for Church union is not denominations but nations, not the Church as such, but the Church for the World."[8]

2. At first sight it seems more or less evident that exceptions to the rules are permitted in unforeseen cases of emergency. This we have known for a long time: emergencies have no law.

On second thought, however, questions arise that we do not get rid of easily and that we certainly cannot answer quickly. For: which emergency can it be that the church has not foreseen? What has to happen to fall outside the normal order and so outside the ready-made paragraphs?

The church is promised a Cross-road by her Lord. Oppression, hatred, discord, are held out in prospect for her; possible imprisonment, flight, dispersion, and persecution are really reckoned with. For a small flock of sheep knowing itself to be sent into the midst of the wolves, emergencies cannot be a surprise. This all belongs to the normal scope of the church. And it is precisely this which people have in mind when they speak about abnormal relations in which extraordinary measures may be taken. They then indeed think of refugees and church-in-diaspora, of people in concentration camps and congregations under the cross; of pariahs, who really have not received more than their Master, who had no place to put his head; in short, of all those categories which cannot be put in the framework of church order and which for this reason must be left free. Here also can abnormalization of the normal take place.

It is unquestionably true that in almost all cases of emergency mentioned above relaxation of strict rules has taken place more than once. Whenever the history of the church-in-emergency might be written, it would become apparent that Intercommunion—without a bad conscience and joyfully—has been celebrated countless times in the dark, while it was still taboo to do the same thing in the light of day. About those facts there can be no uncertainty, I believe.

But it is different with the evaluations of these data; that usually remains ambiguous: wavering between continued hesitation and a convulsive glossing over. The "history of realities" has difficulty here in making connection with the "history of ideas"; events are called "unique" and so are isolated and kept outside the formulas; all things seem to be lined up to prevent the facts from ever being seen as precedents. The emergency at hand may not be evaluated as a continuum, as something "we will have always with us," like the poor; they have to remain occasional, incidental, and marginal cases; no state of emergency but only scattered cases of emergency, which we have to overcome in the form of isolated and casuistically treated items. Our handling of them never touches our "principles." To express it in a formula that has become well known: by way of an "administrative action to meet a temporary situation without prejudice to any principle of ecclesiastical order."[9] Presently this strange infringement on our routine will be past and we shall return to the order of the day.

It probably always will remain a riddle as to how we got into this strange way of thinking. But there should be no doubt that we, with regard to the Biblical sources, have gone through a precarious pseudomorphosis. Presumably a Christianity, bourgeois to its roots, has played tricks on us: a longing for ideologically secured stability, which we in the end found in canonical law; a blueprint of the future, in which there is a guarantee that it all will remain as it was; the desire to keep mastery of the situation—and that was possible only if we humiliated the emergency into something merely casual; belittled the mystery as "a temporary situation," so that it could not rival our mastery. If there is any truth in this hypothesis, which suggests a connection between the curious suppression of the (normal) emergency and the style of living of what we choose to call in shorthand "the Christian establishment," there is hope. Because all of us discover that this establishment is drawing to an end. Our stability-thinking is being traversed by a scurried mobility; church-in-diaspora becomes an everyday phenomenon; where we shall be tomorrow no one can suspect, since we are taken up in *"une civilisation de l'exode"* (Rétif), an exodus culture, which travels away from the old institutions. We do not need to think exclusively of refugee barracks or concentration camps; we have all become "barracks people" (Marcel). Perhaps the emergency does not immediately take on dramatic and spectacular forms; (although?) perhaps we now have to translate suppression and persecution with the modern word "estrangement"—but it is absolutely impossible to point our finger to some particular cases of emergency. We have all fallen in a constant state of emergency. The society that is presupposed in canonical law exists only in a few surviving areas—for the rest it is rank in the brains of the canonists—but not in Main Street *anno* 1963. There, too, many exceptions out of the old books have become common facts of life. What has been judged abnormal for a long time is becoming normal again.

When we, in our changed situation, have to hold to the old line of conduct, we shall have to ask ourselves soberly how this can be applied today. The line of conduct (not the principle) is: dispensation can be given from each (!) rule where it becomes necessary (*ex necessitate cogente, pro necessitate*), after having thoroughly dealt with the facts of each case, until the state of emergency has been taken away.[10]

Question: What happens in a state of emergency, of which the end is not in sight and in which not only individuals but, for instance, a whole generation live? Which pastoral breakthrough of the rules may then be expected? Concretely: Which dispensation may our generation expect, now that she is forced to continue the emergency of the God-dishonoring shame of the divided Communion? This question is not out of order in this rubric: In history a case of emergency often has come into existence when church people were deprived of the pastoral care of their own priests/pastors; sometimes they suddenly remembered that God had more people in town and joined them, perforce, and often also for the sake of Communion. This continued until their own ministers were again available. That was allowed: *ex necessitate cogente.* Would it not be allowed to ask the question here whether the real emergency did not start after the "emergency Intercommunion" had ended and again different closed Communion services were held next to and over against each other in which Christ was fragmentized anew (I Cor. 1:13)? Is it not an irresponsible risk to continue this untenable situation which makes one lose one's faith? Is it impossible to do something here *ad hoc,* possibly without "prejudice to any principle of ecclesiastical order"? Or did we already and simply degrade this constant state of emergency into one of the unsolved ecumenical problems?

3. On death, of course, our rules break to pieces. From the ultimate all the means that try to keep us denominationally divided and apart are suspended. In *periculo mortis* law has to yield to grace: then we often (but still not always) open the doors for all who were emphatically excluded. At that extreme limit, that which did not succeed before can happen: *in extremis* Intercommunion happens for the first time. And even if we hesitate in the danger of death, our hesitations give way to the *fait accompli.* There are only a very few denominations where a blessing is withheld from the dead one who is not of the familiar stable but still belonging to Jesus' flock. Interburials are a (and sometimes the only) form of Intercommunion that is possible.[11]

Maybe some extremists exist who object even to this bigheartedness, but we do well to think of this third breakthrough of the rules not as a maximum but as a minimum possibility: We should not ask what less can happen, strictly speaking, but what could happen in addition, since in the danger of death the obstacles fall away which keep us separate in our life (and as is said: rightly so!). Or with the words of Lund 1952: we now have to try for this concrete case "to reexamine our practice in the light of the exceptions which are already customary."

The first question will have to be whether in this way of thinking death is not given a significance for which the Christian church cannot really take responsibility. Because she knows that death is played out; without "terror." On Easter morning people in the Middle Ages could sing joyfully: "Death, I laugh at thee"!

To repeat the often used words once again: In the scope of our lives death has also become a normal element; it does not distinguish itself as something extraordinary for which extraordinary measures have to be taken; *media vita in morte sumus;* or in the version of Martin Luther: *"Miten wir im Leben sind / von dem Tod umfangen."* If it is true that death still possesses so much majesty that even the "holy" law has to bow for him, then this is not only valid presently, just before the curtain falls, but surely also today, *media vita.* He has already become our silent companion anyway. That we have discovered again. On hearing *periculum mortis* hardly anybody will think of a deathbed or another finale for which one can prepare oneself carefully. This seems to be present only in the minds of the canonists when they speak about the danger of death. But we, we associate it with H-bombs and the forthcoming destruction of the world. And the churches know that, too, whenever they speak of disarmament. The question is whether this changed attitude with regard to life and death should not have far-reaching consequences for permissible relaxations of strict rules. Because we are *in extremis.*

D. Eschatology: the New Overpowers the Old

Until now we have moved within the traditional framework where the question on the mutual relation between rules and exceptions had to be put. We could not escape that. We shall always have to begin in this given context if our speaking does not want to become a wild shot in the air. The question is now whether we can get a step farther. Do we have a chance to pass this stymied debate in such a way that we, on the one hand, take into account as much as we can the intentions of an age-old debate, without, on the other hand, being imprisoned and trapped by the classic arguments?

This would probably succeed if we could place the whole question in a clear eschatological perspective. We do not need magic formulas for that task, and neither should we expect that ready-made solutions will be the immediate result; but perhaps there will be a bit more space in which we can be freed from our orthodox cramps and from the compulsion of the canonical paragraphs. The eschatological theme was introduced in the foregoing when we spoke about mission, emergency, and death. Somewhat prematurely we suggested that these elements are normal for the Christian. Over against the tendency to abnormalize, which we found in the churches, this was necessary. But now the truth must come out: this all is normal because it forms an integrated part of the eschatological existence. We could speak about the missionary situation as we did only because our starting point was that mission is an eschatological *datum* par excellence. (Also literally: *datum* = gift); we had to speak about emergency as we did because we did not understand this only as human misery, but understood it as Messianic suffering in which the advent of the new order is already painfully annunciated; and we could think normally and without excitement about death because we had drawn him already in the circle of light of the resurrection.

In other words we have continuously talked from back to front; from the *coming* future we talked about the *existing* situation; from the new we sought our way to the old. For that is what matters with eschatology: not that we round off history with a terrific climax, but that we learn to deal freely with the whole of time. In such a way that the past cannot exercise power anymore, for it is conquered, we can only "remember it in joy." In such a way that the present does not become a dead-end alley in which we get caught, but the supreme moment in which a way is offered to us on which we indeed can go. In such a way that the future does not any longer seem like a dull repetition of what has been before, but turns out to be the open space of freedom which we can enter with confidence and great expectation. In short, eschatology is: the new already has evident surplus value and for that reason more and more overpowers the old.

New is here the sum total of all that has broken into this world with Jesus, that *"Avantgardist* of the new era" (Stauffer): the Kingdom and the Spirit; the freedom for service in solidarity and the restoration of humanity; salvation and peace—and all the rest. All of this is not on the same chronological scale as what was before, but it proclaims the definite end to the old world. Jesus does not turn a page in the book of time, he definitely closes the book forever; out of that book there is nothing to be told anymore; the times are "full" (Gal. 4:4; Eph. 1:10). That is to say: finished is the way of living in which we tried to perpetuate ourselves through religion and law; there is no future for the closed order in which a fixed place was allotted to everybody and everything; this whole business has become an anachronism. In Jesus, people are introduced into an unprecedented history of free men, a continuous risky adventure with always hazardous improvisations; each year is a new venture without model or example; of each of the years that we count from Jesus Christ, we only know that it will be a "year of our Lord" and that must suffice. Now then, *"When anyone is united with Christ, there is a new world; the old order has gone, the new order has already begun."* (II Cor. 5:17.) I think that here lies the heart of the eschatological existence. A new act of creation[12] has taken us out of the oppression of our closed and too little world and put us in open history with wide horizons, in the middle of ultimate realities, which Jesus directs toward us from the ultimate. Only the man who is open toward *this* future is up to date; only he who expects that this new reality not only has evident surplus value over the old today, but also that it will again get superiority over it, only he deserves to be called sanguine.

In this climate (of living and not only of thinking) the different questions that we have dealt with above get a new face and in any case a new weight: Communion as an eschatological Sacrament is the representation of the Kingdom in the *world;* it is impossible to lock up the Kingdom in the church, and it is equally impossible to make this Sacrament of the Kingdom a purely churchly event. Finally, Intercommunion is not a question between denominations but between nations; not of Intercommunion between all sorts of confessions but between people of all sorts. Communion is the first fulfillment ("The new order has already begun!") of the "feast that the Lord will make for all nations" (Isa. 25:6). So plans and practices of Intercommunion will have to be extended to the "many [= all nations?] for whom the blood of the covenant was already shed" (Matt. 26:28).

What has to happen concretely in the perspective of the meal of the nations, which the Lord is preparing, is not so easily prescribed in one single prescription. Of course, we are not very serious about it when, as has happened in the last years in certain parts of the world, we only strengthen our "eschatological parts" in the liturgy of the Eucharist and leave all other things as they were. We are only beginning to move in this perspective when everything is done at every celebration of Communion to communicate with the non- (not anymore and not yet) communicants, *from wherever they come*. Thus we are working on more basic questions than the eternal issue as to how the communicants of one denomination can be put together "in peace and order" with the communicants of another denomination.

The order for the celebration of the eschatological Sacrament of Communion must as a matter of course be an *eschatological order:* that is to say, open-ended and so structured that we can have this order "as if we did not have it." That is now clear. We can shut off nothing to the front of us, as if we could dispose of the future in any way. The way toward the future must be kept open for "signs and miracles," which we expect since the new order has already begun; there always has to be a place for surprise. For instance, for the surprise that Christians of different traditions, who are communicating often with those outside, suddenly start having Intercommunion, even when the valid rules do not make this possible. (We see it happen!) For such manifestations (of the Spirit?) there must be a place in any order, simply because we do not know beforehand exactly how the Lord wants to visit his people. No closed-ended order; we have enough trouble with that because all our confessions are saddled with an order that only reflects the situation of a pre-ecumenical age. (Also the ecumenical movement is such a surprise of the Spirit, which found us unprepared and for which we had hardly any space in our order.)

This of course also has a bearing on the structure of the order itself. Since this structure is an open-ended one, it gets a somewhat provisional and even floating character.[13] A definite fixation is out of the question. Like all other things we received in the eschatological existence, we shall also "have our order as if we did not have it"; prepared to use it, at a hint of the Spirit, and to apply it, but also prepared, at a hint of the same Spirit, to ignore it and let it go.

And so we have finally expressed the fact that in the eschatological climate this whole somewhat convulsive distinction between rules and exceptions is quite dubious, between principles and (temporary) administrative actions, between strict application of canonical law and a pastorally responsible breakthrough of that same law. We can only decide *ad hoc* on what should happen: in the moment and in the situation where "tradition" takes place, which according to the roots of the word means where and when God wills that his Son is tradited; handed over, given away (Matt. 17:22), delivered over into the hands of men (Rom. 8:31). What actually happens when Jesus Christ is tradited to men breaks through all systematization. When anyone is united with Christ—there is a new act of creation.

When we still want to say something about rules, it has to happen in such a loose way that we are threatened with the greatest confusion of tongues: we can only speak of that sort of rule which is never applied strictly but always "economically"; rules that form an unbreakable unity with their exceptions: it is the same Lord who rules and excepts, and it is the same Spirit whom it pleases sometimes to work according to our expectations, which we hold on account of our earlier experiences (we had already made rules out of them), and who on other occasions surprises us with new, unexpected turns. Perhaps there is still too much of the old order (which has gone!) in this way of thinking about rules and exceptions; too much desire to live through the new time in the categories of the old time; history in the way of the closed order; the future as the past projected forward; the hints of the Spirit, who according to his nature cannot stop doing new things, as rules in which we want to see the old experience confirmed —and behind this all: perhaps in this way of thinking there is still too much of a safety-first desire, which is the core of all religiosity. But that is put "off side" once and for all in the coming of Jesus.

In a delightful book about the work of the Holy Spirit, the author confesses that he seriously contemplated entitling his work, which is now called *God in Action,* as "Safety Last." "Wiser, or more cautious, counsel prevailed. But it will probably have been sufficiently clear that Safety Last has been the dominant note throughout."[14] That belongs intrinsically together: God in Action—The Holy Spirit—Safety Last: and it would be precious if we would discover this relation with regard to our Intercommunion discussions, in which often the smallest risk possible is immediately killed by the greatest responsibility possible. As if the servants, sent out to the main thoroughfares to invite everyone they can find, had to act as the bodyguards protecting the Lord of Hosts, who has already begun to prepare the feast for all nations. (86.)

X

ON THE WAY TO
THE WORLD OF TOMORROW

"CREATIVE RATS AND THE SINKING SHIP" is the title of a chapter in a stimulating book called *Early Christians of the 21st Century*.[1] A vision of the future. Hazardous. Postmodern society is sketched in a few lines, without illusion or bombast or sentimental reiterations.

The author has carefully observed the "creative rats" that he sees today leaving the ship—What are they thinking? What are they doing? What are they looking for?—and he lets them show him where we are heading: the twenty-first century. This, then, is the world of the day after tomorrow.

Before we get there we shall have to go through the nightmares of *1984,* whether they proceed from the feverish mind of Orwell and others or from the cool deliberation of younger colleagues among the guild of prophets. I think of someone like Hartley, who recently unveiled "The New State": instituted after the Third World War; populated by "patients and delinquents" who go in sackcloth and ashes because of their fault, their own fault, their own most grievous fault; a standardized mass of humanity without any name or individual face; but in whom resistance nevertheless comes alive, though only in the heart of a single person (Jael 97, a woman in Hartley's book), and the plan is made to cast off the tyranny.[2]

A little nearer we face *Utopia 1976*.[3] A world like the model kitchen in the *Ladies' Home Journal:* pastel-colored, perfect, comfortable, clean, sterile, deadly dull; and above it, a cupola, and a heaven (whatever for?), in glaring colors; something like a cosmic jukebox, which the whole day long "plugs" religion into the universe: is this, then, to be the "heaven" of tomorrow?

Nearer home, on our very doorstep, we find all kinds of guesses about what tomorrow will be. A cautious groping for "The Shape of the Future"[4]; a preliminary sketch of the atomic age which we have just entered[5]; a somewhat premature X-ray photograph of "Modern Man and His Future"[6]; even "The Landmarks of Tomorrow" have already been revealed to us, but this was certainly done too rashly and we are now told that what we see in these landmarks is not the future but the "palpable today."[7] What shall we do with all these visions of the world of tomorrow?

It is impossible to put them together. They are not parts of a puzzle that fit to form a complete panorama. These dreams projected into the future are too heterogeneous, and all these freely scattered prophecies differ too much one from the other. And this could indeed be a first important insight: apparently it is not so evident what exactly will come. *The future remains open.* Many things are possible.

"Tomorrow" is not the secretly set fishnet into which we shall all inevitably swim and be caught. Nor is it the secret trap where the soothsayers are already thronging in anticipation of the general downfall. "Tomorrow" is still only a half-explored country, which has yet to be shown to us.

Herewith we have begun to open the way. At least we have left behind some common images that time and again threaten to entangle and immobilize us.

For instance, we have for a long time been saying that only pessimists look into the future. Optimists have given up,[8] apparently with good reason. For there seems not much in the coming tomorrow that could make us happy.

We are given the impression that the central theme of

the world of tomorrow is already fixed—namely, "Man is dead." And we still may cleverly compose variations on this theme, discuss it either in a veiled manner or in a brutal and exaggerated way, but it is impossible for us to change it. The theme has been fixed once for all. Usually one adds a "revealing" comment. The nineteenth century dared to proclaim through the mouth of its most daring prophets that "God is dead." This was done with the "pathos" of an evangelist; a "dysangelist," said Rosenstock. One can almost see him climb up the hill, put the trumpet to his lips, demanding a hearing, and when silence has fallen proclaim throughout the whole universe "God is dead!" Terrified, man composed a high-church liturgy for the funeral procession. The deceased was buried with long, intoned litanies.

Now look at the difference: we in the twentieth century do not proclaim, we just mention the fact that man is dead. It is a laconic statement made on the terrace over an aperitif; a fragment of boulevard philosophy: "Man is dead—anybody got a cigarette?"

No formal, elaborate service is needed here—the old fossil is buried in as simple and low-church a manner as possible[9], with no more than a four-line cabaret song. Even the one by Bert Brecht sounds too pathetic and too old-fashioned for our ears:

> Praised be the chill, the darkness and the doom.
> Look up and see!
> You do not count,
> and you can die without worrying.[10]

This cultural pessimism has penetrated our pores to such an extent that we hardly notice how selective and one-sided we have become. For, if we look around us without any prejudice, we suddenly discover yet quite different traveling companions on the journey to the world of tomorrow. It may well be that poets have become "dysangelists" with regard to the future of mankind, and dreamers see only cemeteries ahead, but there is also that strange column of scientists marching along with us. Happily they prove to us with their formulas that the wholesale rebirth of humanity is just at hand. A great emancipation is on our doorstep. One last effort and we can finish off the present "hominoid" era. A little more perseverance and the machine will have liberated man from the machine, and finally we shall be able to "specialize in the human."[11] Tomorrow we shall experience the resurrection of mankind. And there is the end of that central theme which we supposed was given to us.

So it is indeed a curious caravan in which we are traveling. Definitely not an army under only one flag. Rather, an almost amorphous mass with diffused ideas. Optimist and pessimist march shoulder to shoulder. Alongside the utopian marches courageously the new figure of the "metopian"—the man who regards all thinking about the future as self-deception and so much waste of time. In each blueprint of the future he can see nothing except a carrot dangling in front of the donkey which draws the cart of history. In this way, we may well advance, but in a rather unsporting way! Therefore: do not proclaim a promised land; get rid of attractive utopias that are furnished with our dreams and populated with our ideals—be a man and ignore the future, Metopia! There may be no other place than where I stand today; no land other than where I live today; no alibi. And with an angry gesture the door of the world to come is slammed shut.

We must take sober account of all these varied conceptions. Therefore don't evaluate and choose too quickly. Continue to listen with discernment both to the left and to the right without falling for either. Accept what cannot yet be perceived, do not flee from what is still ambiguous —certainly *not* into that all too familiar pseudo-pious flight ahead, over the world of tomorrow and into another world where no problems exist. For the ultimate meets us in the pre-ultimate, or temporal. And the Lord who comes toward us (and as such is our future) wants to visit us in those dark (or light?) years of 1976 or 1984.

If we now prepare to go ahead, we see that, after all, something of what awaits us is already known: the world of tomorrow is already present. *Tomorrow is here.* The people of tomorrow have become our contemporaries. Together with them we make up the post-modern society which—almost imperceptibly—made its entry some twenty-five years ago. Those who still want to be "modern" have become old-fashioned. They are a quarter of a century behind the times.

As we look around discerningly, we can somehow form an idea of what is to come. About two things we shall quickly come to agree: we shall have to cross cataracts of time, turn another page, and live in discontinuity with the life of yesterday. The great slogans of modern man—continuity and progress—have been changed by post-modern man into *change* ("change will be the only unchangeable") and *renewal.* And this again implies facing a period of fundamental *uncertainty.* Already the secure ones are suspected and ruled out as an anachronism, and soon what we do will become more obviously a risky adventure: simply because we do not have time to get the necessary information in order to act wisely. What information we finally get will repeatedly prove to be too little, too late. Therefore, the many who give us information about the world of tomorrow urge us to play down our longing for certainty and to endure the uncertainty without panic and fear; to accept what is risky, to live by improvisation, and to experiment.[12]

After all these general comments it would be foolish to give a full-dress discourse. We can do no more than offer some tentative suggestions, some guesses and hopes that spring from the tomorrow which is already here; some preliminary reconnoitering—of course quite controversial!

What I now want to put before you for consideration are some notes under four headings: What Must We Leave

Behind Us on Our Way to the World of Tomorrow?; Life as World Citizens; Ecumenical Diaspora; The Desert as the Promised Land.

A. WHAT MUST WE LEAVE BEHIND US?

The world of tomorrow may well be present already; nevertheless, we can still refuse to enter it. The normal fear of crossing the threshold can easily be overcome. More difficult for us will be to deal with that plot against the future, that widespread conspiracy, which wants to leave everything as it is. The clever politics of the ostrich, which always leads us to put our head into the traditional sand ("we don't see anything new"); the fervent marking time that is so reassuring ("we're progressing nicely, aren't we!"); and also that ingenious invention that we have copied from an American egghead: every day he takes off in his plane and sets his course so as to land where it is still yesterday. If I am not mistaken, this figure has quite a few followers in our circle. You can see it on a rather large scale: we take off in 1960 with a whole cargo of slogans about renewal and projects for the future; one would say we were bound to go in the right direction; but we still manage to set our course so as to land, for instance, about 325 (*Corpus Christianum*), or around 800 (parochial system), or precisely in 1517 (Reformation). You can see it in all possible ways, on a small scale also: for instance, we go searching for a *new* song (as we say) and then set course for the Bach airport, or just manage to make an (emergency?) landing on Gregorian soil.

No, we can only really enter the new world if we dare, quite deliberately, choose tomorrow (and this means that if necessary we must deliberately choose against today and yesterday); if we dare to see and experience our journey as nothing less than an exodus. And then at once we are faced with the question of what has to be left behind in the old country. What is the content of the fleshpots of Egypt that have to be discarded? Simply because it is no longer suitable as traveling rations, because it would burden us unnecessarily and slow down our progress; but also because it is in itself a constant temptation to hark back and be enslaved by nostalgia and homesickness. So, what must be left behind?

1. First of all, I think we must leave behind all that constitutes the "yesterday-in-concreto": this lumping together of practical knowledge and experience which, among other things, has manifested itself in current methodology and techniques. We encounter this in social work, but for instance also in practical theology, which—in its traditional form—is not much more than the communication of the ecclesiastical "yesterday-in-concreto." It is quite natural that *this* tradition should be less and less appropriate and relevant: it is too directly related to the situation in the old country which has been left, too strongly orientated toward Egypt, and it will therefore fail us increasingly as we journey farther on. And this happens precisely in a period in which—impressed by the complexity of our society—we have become so afraid of improvisation. What we want is a clear recipe; the "tip"—frozen experience; an approach that really works. Yet we shall not get that recipe and we should stop asking for it; the tip can at best give us an impression of how things once were; and we ourselves must find the approach.

Now, all this need not confuse us unduly: have we not always claimed that our methods are only preliminary and are of course capable of variation according to the situation? Have we not always claimed to be ready to review and examine them critically step by step? In principle therefore, we are on the right track. But am I mistaken if I say that—now that it really matters, now that the marker buoys have to be moved—again and again we behave as damned "methodists"? [NOTE: Obviously the author does not refer here to a particular Christian denomination but to all those who believe in methods (Ed.).] Quite willing to alter some things now and again, but not ready for any radical change? The "yesterday-in-concreto" still continues to overpower us, and to let us go (really go?) through life as prisoners chained to history.

What then shall we do? It seems to me that we have to cultivate a healthy skepticism toward all traditional forms and procedures; we must prevent ourselves being hypnotized by familiarity. Therefore we must put the fundamental questions: not begin halfway with the question *"How* shall we continue to do in the future what we used to do in Egypt?" (for instance, *how* shall we have to preach?), but we must begin to ask the basic question *whether* the dear old (and perhaps sacred?) way can and must be continued in the future ("shall we in fact still preach?"). Yet again: if we leave behind us the yesterday-in-concreto, those who are its guardians and transmitters will fade into the background: the older generation. In order really to enter into the situation of tomorrow the younger generation will have to be given a generously free hand. They must have the chance (or else they should take it) to break step, to find a new rhythm without our being annoyed, or pointing admonishing fingers and also, please, without scandalized protests from the old "watchdogs." The seriousness with which we opt for tomorrow will, to a great extent, show itself in the confidence we place in the younger generation, and therefore also for instance in our readiness to put younger men into leading positions (in which so many jubilees are celebrated).

2. We must also bid farewell to the *pattern of society* to which we have gradually become accustomed. During these last years it has been difficult enough for us to progress from the "neighborhood communities" in which we had worked for centuries to the "work communities" where we have barely learned the first steps. In various ways we have tried to force a breakthrough from the "leisure-time" sector to the "work" sector. This can be seen clearly in the annals of the lay training centers. And now, when we have really begun, we are told that a society is at hand in which

THE WORLD OF TOMORROW

questions of work become considerably less important
and urgent: "a society that will be less industrial than any
we have ever experienced since the beginning of the industrial revolution."[13] Compared with working hours (the
sphere of our "first vocation"), our leisure will become
quantitatively and qualitatively so important that now it is
already suggested that we should be more concerned about
the "sphere of our second vocation."[14]

True, it is rather annoying, but much of what we have
quite recently discovered about the place and task of the
church in industrial society[15] will also have to be discarded.
And these newly acquired insights that are so enthusi-
astically reported, and so fanatically propagated, will prove
to be of little relevance in the world of tomorrow. Perhaps
they may still have some importance for just one small
sector of life.

Meanwhile, we shall have to prepare ourselves for a
realistic confrontation with the problem that will soon be
facing us critically in the leisure society: the problem of
unending boredom. I do not know whether it is true that by
1976 no one will be interested anymore in a discussion
about immortality but will only become animated over the
question of how to pass the time on a wet day off.[16] But
we may quite safely suppose that the perplexity which already faces many people when yet another Sunday is before
them will soon extend over a long weekend; this "weekly
yawn" will then last for days; this dread and helpless anger
at the prospect of "empty time," referred to in the popular
songs (*Je hais le dimanche*) will then spread like an oil
stain; and the "one-day neurosis" that many people already
suffer from will then be a weekend neurosis.

This therefore involves gearing in to a new type of society, which can no longer be understood or defined by
using the old categories. It will be necessary to search at
least as seriously for ways to enter the sphere of the second vocation as we have sought for ways to enter the first
vocation. This means in practice that, besides the parochial

neighborhood communities, we shall have to experiment with untrammeled imagination in the creation of a far greater diversity of types of communities, in the "work" sector *and* in the "boredom sector" for the "leisure-time nomads," and the curbside tourists.

3. Among the fleshpots of Egypt that have to be left behind must be counted (in my mind) all that is embodied in the term "Christendom": a very involved, complicated structure about which we can here make only a few comments. It cannot be denied that "Christendom" was a most important cultural factor in our history. It would be ungrateful, unworthy, and unnecessary to contradict this fact, to deny or even to minimize it. Whether we know it or not, we are surrounded by "the decencies and charities of Christendom" (Chesterton). And we live with it. Christian fingerprints are still to be found somewhere in almost all our institutions and patterns, usually still recognizable as such (although the trained eye of the detective becomes ever more necessary).

In the world of tomorrow this "yesterday" cannot be undone, but it is possible to dismiss it from our minds as something that is over and done with. If the signs do not mislead us, this is what will happen: Christendom will be assigned the role of the Moor who has done his duty (and badly, at that); now he can go. And indeed, the Moor has gone! Just look: all that is left of the whole, in itself perhaps impressive, "Christian" history is this end product, a post-Christian, secularized society. It is this which we face today. Any "Christian values" that may still be current will inevitably be gathered together tomorrow under the heading "sentimentalities."[17]

Perhaps it is unnecessary to remind ourselves in passing that religion has no place in the baggage we take on our journey to "tomorrow." Of course not; for it is quite clearly something belonging to "yesterday." Twenty centuries ago it was once for all left behind and became definitely outdated. After the cross, there was no more future for religion; it was filed in the Past Historic. It is utterly pointless to attempt to take it out again or to try to refurbish it for further use. We can with a clear conscience disregard religion, and any relics of it that still remain to remind us of it may be shown up as something that has now really had its day.

What about the churches' way of life? It will be asking for trouble to inquire how much of that can and must be left behind. For here we really walk on holy ground, into the company of intolerant ax-grinders. As soon as the "structures of the church" come under discussion we discover to our great astonishment that there are still inquisitors and heresy hunters around who are seeking for their prey. There is a rumor[18] that they justify their strange activity on the ground of an emended text of Paul: "Now there remaineth faith, hope, and charity, these three, but the greatest of these is the *status quo*."

Let us nevertheless take the risk: it seems to me that we shall also have to leave behind the *Volkskirche* [national church] and practically everything involved in this term. Church statistics give us enough food for thought, although we need not yet bow before mere numbers. Yet if we not only count souls but also plumb the depths of the present situation, it becomes ever more clear how few real opportunities the church has to function as a formative power for a whole nation. To do this, the base has become too narrow—and meanwhile, apparently, the "progressive reduction of the milieu" continues relentlessly.[19] With the exception of perhaps a few remaining areas, we may count less and less on conventional "churchliness." This, among other things, implies also that each denomination (whatever its pretensions in church order) begins to show the marks of a "gathered" or "voluntary" church, in which decisions are required step by step: first, the decision to break with the "unchurchliness" which has now become a convention; afterward, the constantly repeated decision to remain within the church despite all the pressure of society. For such a situation the *Volkskirche* is barely prepared: in general it has become a framework within which the "religion without decision" is nurtured, upheld, and propagated; institutionalized indecision.[20] Without fundamental changes of structure (through which it would cease to be a *Volkskirche*) it has become unusable.

Almost always the *Volkskirche* implies also a missionary program. The intention was: a church that exists for the whole of society, and that indeed is directed toward its total context. In accordance with the nineteenth-century conception, this context was a baptized *Volk* (nation).

That missionary program must stand uncut. As the vehicle of the gospel that seeks to reach the ends of the world, the church can never question its universal intention without losing its own self. This must also be made clear in the terms of today. The word *Volkskirche* had then better be forgotten: it is too provincial; it suggests that the church prefers cautiously to respect national frontiers rather than to cross them boldly; it contradicts the very thing it was meant to say; namely, that the church exists for the *world*. On the way to tomorrow, we must single-mindedly think and act with nothing less in mind than the total oikoumene (the whole world). Because, there is surely no uncertainty about this, that on our way we shall have to train ourselves in *life as world citizens*.

B. LIFE AS WORLD CITIZENS

It is not so long ago that the whole world was joined together in one single historic framework. We have only just accustomed ourselves to this fact and still find it very hard to live within this one context, within these universal relationships.

Of course, officially we have ruled the final line under the Vasco da Gama era. A formal witch-hunt has been started against the remnants of European-centered thinking, now regarded as utterly outdated. We can scarcely speak about

colonialism in other than derogatory terms: this foolish
claim to have assigned to ourselves (unasked) the role of
"lord and master" and to all others, naturally, that of
"servants," has become plainly ridiculous. Those who have
ears can hear this proclaimed from the housetops. Here
and there, indeed, we seem to have got off our high horse
and onto ordinary ground level. But let us not deceive
ourselves: emotionally Europe is still felt to be a great
myth rather than an ordinary continent. Whenever possible,
we rejoice with Europe as it wags its mythical tail. This
appears, for instance, whenever Europe still demands
special privileges for herself and sets herself apart in this
way from the rest of the world. The sentimental pathos
with which this often happens does not suggest that we are
merely busy with the liquidation of affairs passed on to
us from an earlier generation.

Spasmodically we try to stretch the past and to add a
twenty-fifth hour to the day that is definitely over. This
often appears when we use, so emphatically, that slippery
camouflage term "the West": the West, which apparently
is endowed with a special "missionary calling," or which
so urgently wants to enter into "a dialogue with the East";
as if we had still not reached the Great Society, in which
East and West continually gear into each other and color
each other so that they can no longer be put one over
against the other as partners in dialogue.

The most dangerous manifestation of the old superiority
complex occurs when the European enters the scene as
what the Bible would call "a rich man": somebody who is
really somebody and who thinks that he can prove it;
draped around him he displays his impressive possessions
(culture, technics, spending power). He has everything—
except a contrite heart.

If we want to take our normal place in the world community, we shall have to carry through to its conclusion
the disenchantment (*Entzauberung*) of Europe, the West,

from myth to quite ordinary continent. This means also that we have to give up our privileged positions: our "domination" (in this respect much has already been done) and our "wealth" (in this respect I think we have still to begin). The world of tomorrow, seen as a whole, can only be a *poor* world. For the moment, one cannot yet reckon on "welfare for all." Assistance to countries of rapid social change can only very modestly aim at "raising the standard *toward* poverty"; it can only just help to pass the threshold of man-worthy (but still pauper) existence; at best, a minimum existence for all can be reached. Solidarity with this world, therefore, can be nothing else than solidarity in poverty. And the genuineness of our desire for this must be proved in the self-discipline that we dare to impose upon ourselves: our restriction of ourselves to a minimum and our readiness to share liberally with others all that is at our disposal. To my mind, this demands of the church that it empty itself to become the church-of-the-poor.[21] As a middle-class church it not only lives above its means, but it also isolates itself from the fabric of this world. Perhaps its self-discipline might require that—to begin with—it use not more of its available potential (manpower, money, etc.) for itself than it cedes to others. This, of course, sounds foolishly unrealistic; but I cannot conceive how the attempt to return to the secret of the church-of-the-poor can, by all relevant criteria, ever seem to be anything else than "foolish" and "unrealistic." Probably we shall be helped a step farther if we try to get an idea of the position in which Christianity will find itself in the world of tomorrow. The population explosion, which is already a fact and which we shall still have to expect, will fundamentally alter the numerical relationship between Christians and non-Christians. In international missionary circles this whole change is often summarized in one single short sentence: "The Church is, in fact, now pursuing its mission at a time when the birth rate is fast outstripping the conversion rate."[22]

For once one dares to give some figures: for instance, 1900: Christians—34 percent of the world population; 1955: 31 percent; 2000: 16 percent. The latter figure is, of course, more a (modest) article of faith than a sound statistical fact. But, even if we do not insist precisely on these figures, the trend is quite clear: in the world of tomorrow Christianity will become an ever-decreasing minority. We may continue to hope for pleasant surprises but still meanwhile reckon soberly with this development and prepare ourselves for it.

C. Ecumenical Diaspora

This preparation will be all the more necessary since we can expect the shrinking process of Christianity already mentioned to change relationships fundamentally on the universal scale, and also in some regional and local situations, for instance in Europe. It appears that here indeed the long period of "multitudinism" has passed. The great and compact church units have broken apart into many small groups: minorities in their own milieu. This has happened under the pressure from outside (Eastern Europe) or, less dramatically, through the continuous "erosion" of local church life.[23] Long ago, therefore, perceptive minds based their strategy of building up the local congregation on small "nuclei, cells, teams," or whatever they may be called—and they gave up shallow talk about "our big church with its millions of members."

If no unexpected changes occur in the world of tomorrow, the churches will find themselves again clearly in a *diaspora* situation: living in dispersion as thinly spread minority groups. Toynbee advises us therefore—as a mental training for what is to come—to study the Jewish diaspora again seriously.[24] The first thing we have to do, it seems to me, is nothing else than *to accept the diaspora;* without bitterness and resentment, without attempting to escape into a dream that has passed, a romantic fiction, or a clever plan for the formation of new church blocks, which might after all help us to regain a majority position. In short, we must hear and obey "our call to be a minority."[25]

Our concern must then be to make the small groups steadfast in diaspora (*diasporafest*): holding out against an overpowering environment that tries to squeeze everything into the same mold; with closely knit relationships which nevertheless remain open; an intense communion which yet does not make the group a ghetto; simultaneously completely dedicated (commitment!) and ready for service (*disponibilité*). In the German discussion about this matter still another term is offered to us, borrowed from the German army. The organization of the group must be "foolproof" (*idiotensicher*).

This means: the organization of the group should be so strong in itself that even a fool cannot wreck it. We had better not accept this program. For the church cannot entrench itself in an organization proof against the possible failure of its members. It is its glory that it chooses the vulnerability of its (God's) fools rather than the security promised by the perfect order of things.

In this diaspora situation are probably also our greatest ecumenical opportunities and chances. And as far as I can see, these are not yet sufficiently exploited. Religious sociologists have already quite expressively pointed us to the "training grounds for ecumenical encounter," which we find on our doorstep as more and more members of other churches come to live among us.[26] Yet, often the door remains shut, and frequently enough the training ground becomes a battlefield. Moreover, this is still too much thinking in terms of "blocks"; too much according to the traditional and stable (rural?) patterns; also too obviously starting from the idea that denominations will still remain "established": in a majority position and exempt from the general process of "reduction of Christendom." In short, it savors too much of *Volkskirchen*.

No, I think we must take for granted that our mobile society will stir up all denominations and lead them into dispersion; no one will escape the diaspora. Together we are pushed to the fringe of society in order there to serve as "a proportionally ever decreasing minority." There we shall encounter one another as people who have left their fortified positions and now only vaguely remember those strong and solid houses which they once inhabited—or we shall not meet one another at all; there, on the fringe, we shall recognize each other as "Hebrews"—or we shall not recognize one another at all.

When we engage in ecumenical work (for instance, here in Holland), it often seems that we have never heard of this diaspora. Whenever possible, we should like to deny that fearful and unpredictable event, we should like to annul it or, at least, hold it back as long as possible. We establish ourselves again quite firmly in our houses; true, they become somewhat empty, but at least they are built on a solid foundation; with a park surrounding them. We make friendly signs to our neighbors and visit them from time to time. In all the houses we often and eagerly talk about the Abrahamic adventure and about the people of God (that is, ourselves) on its pilgrimage through the desert. In the midst of our parks we talk about the desert. And meanwhile it appears that our whole enterprise is adversely affected by immobility.[27]

Could it be possible also that our churches have become "houses in Egypt," which we must leave (not only in our talks but in actual fact)? Or have we left already without giving notice? And is it foolish, on the way to the world of tomorrow, into the diaspora, also to consider seriously whether our councils of churches as they are at present allowed to function had not better vanish? They create the illusion that we are already on the way together and they wrongly give us an alibi for our own immobility. Are we ready to accept the dispersion; to accept the fact that so many have already drifted far away from home and can no longer be called back to the stately and static patterns? Must we simply write them off (estranged from the church, therefore nonecumenical: that always rings a bell!)? Or could they perhaps become the pioneers for something new? Spearheads in the ecumenical diaspora who learn to understand their dispersion as a divine call and their living in tents as the possibility of remaining mobile and available? In the coming years these questions must receive a clear answer. Meanwhile, I think we must use, with much imagination and confidence, all ecumenical opportunities inherent in the diaspora situation. Our houses cannot be "talked together." Did we not solemnly declare our desire (Evanston) not to remain nailed to our seats and, whenever it must be, to give up our houses in "an obedience unto death"? Moreover, these houses will probably soon be hardly inhabited anymore. In the tents we shall find each other again, like the Hebrews, abused by all those Egyptians who do not know the difference between a Hebrew and a schismatic or traitor. And this will happen in the desert.

D. THE DESERT AS THE PROMISED LAND

Let us not have any illusions, the way toward the world of tomorrow leads into the desert. I believe that the Biblical story of the exodus will, in a very special way, become our story—even if the outcome is different. Disappointment and setbacks await us, but they are surrounded by a host of signs and miracles. In the drought we shall find an oasis, indeed also Mara, bitter water. And when we dare not expect anything further (Fata Morgana?), suddenly we are surprised by Elim: wells and palm trees, and in the barren land, manna every day anew. Where now we only vaguely and uncertainly detect a track, there will be a path clearly shown to us. What happens along the way will not be so conspicuous. Nothing for the newspapers. Here and there a sign of shalom: reconciliation, peace, joy, freedom. A pennyworth of hope for people who have given up hope. A parcel of desert made inhabitable, a bit of life made human by that incorrigible Humanist, who is well pleased with mankind. We shall gaze in wonder. And in these signs we shall see the future approach: the Lord, who comes toward us and who, according to his promise, will make the desert into the Promised Land.

> The wilderness and the dry land shall be glad,
> The desert shall rejoice and blossom.
>
> (Isa. 35:1.)

Again, let us not have any illusions: the way toward the world of tomorrow leads into the promised land. The situation in which we stand and about which we have our doubts is already imprisoned in the time that is to come; the desert that we may face with anguish will blossom as the rose. It is the place where the new world of tomorrow is on the verge of breaking through. Let us conclude by reminding one another of the psalm that today has given so many young people courage to meet tomorrow/Tomorrow:

> Ye children of Zion, rise up and march—
>   A new time dawns today.
> Prepare the way for Him who comes—
>   A new time dawns today.
> For Satan falls now under His Sword—
>   A new time dawns today.
> Thus law and justice are fulfilled—
>   A new time dawns today.
> The morning star shines in the sky—
>   We now see the new day.   (76.)

NOTES

Chapter I. The Call to Evangelism

1. C. W. Ranson, ed., *Renewal and Advance* (International Missionary Council, 1948), p. 215.

2. E. Kellerhals, "Sind wir noch Pionier-Mission?" *E.M.M.*, 1948, pp. 104 ff.

3. Ecumenical Press Service, Nov. 26, 1948.

4. Cf. F. Laubach, "How to Convert 1,200,000,000 People," in *Church of England Newspaper*, Oct. 7, 1949.

5. Cf. G. Wehrung, *Die Kirche nach evangelischem Verständnis* (1946), pp. 29 ff.

6. *Verbum: unica perpetua et infallibilis ecclesiae nota* (Luther). Cf. E. Wolf, *Evangelische Theologie*, 1938, pp. 134 ff.

7. *Innere Mission*, 1849. "Home missions is that total work, that love born from faith in Christ, which seeks to renew those *multitudes in Christendom* who have fallen prey to the power and the rule of all sorts of lost conditions, which directly or indirectly is the result of sin, but who are not reached by the existing ministries."

8. "Don't, under any conditions, get mixed up in outward things," Utendörfer, *Zinzendorfs Missions Instruktionen* (Herrnhut, 1913), p. 9.

9. In North America, especially David Zeisberger (1720–1808) (among the Indians), and in Antigua, Peter Braun.

10. G. Hermann, *Karl Graul und seine Bedeutung für die lutherische Mission* (Halle, 1867).

11. W. Kunze, *Der Missionsgedanke bei Schleiermacher* (1927); O. Kübler, *Mission und Theologie* (1929); E. zur

Nieden, *Der Missionsgedanke in der systematischen Theologie seit Schleiermacher* (1928).

12. R. Rothe, *Theologische Ethik,* Vol. V, p. 1178.

13. Cf. G. M. Young, ed., *Early Victorian England,* II, 1934, p. 392.

14. J. Dürr, *Sendende und werdende Kirche in der Missions-Theologie G. Warnecks* (Basel, 1947), p. 159.

15. "The expansion of belief in Yaweh among all nations is part of the Messianic expectation," A. G. Hebert, *The Throne of David* (Morehouse-Barlow Co., 1942), p. 72.

16. O. Michel, "Menschensohn und Völkerwelt," *Evangelische Missions Zeitschrift,* 1941, pp. 257 ff.

17. Max Warren, *The Truth of Vision* (London: Canterbury Press, 1948).

18. Cf. O. Cullmann, *Christus und die Zeit* (Zürich, 1946), pp. 138–153. For a Roman Catholic view, see J. Daniélou, *Le Mystère du Salut des Nations* (1945), pp. 85–110.

19. Cf. J. Pedersen, *Israel* I–II (Oxford University Press, Vol. I, 1926; Vol. II, 1940), pp. 311 ff.

20. E. Stauffer, *Die Theologie des N. T.* (Geneva, 1945), p. 123.

21. P. Minear, *The Eyes of Faith* (The Westminster Press, 1945), p. 267.

22. Warren, *op. cit.,* p. 57.

23. M. Kähler, *Dogmatische Zeitfragen,* II, pp. 347–351; H. Frick, *Mission und Propaganda* (1927).

24. H. A. van Andel, *De zendingsleer van G. Voetius* (1912). Here and there is added *conversio gentium.*

25. J. Merle Davis, *New Buildings on Old Foundations* (International Missionary Council, 1945).

26. C. H. Dodd, *The Apostolic Preaching and Its Developments* (Harper & Row, Publishers, Inc., 1936).

27. *International Review of Missions,* Oct. 1949, pp. 407–408.

28. D. T. Jenkins, "A Message to Ministers About the Communication of the Gospel," *Theology Today,* 1949, pp. 183–184.

29. Cf. Report of Bossey Conference on Evangelism, March, 1949.

30. R. Loew, *En Mission Prolétarienne* (1946).
31. Similar to what W. Temple called "social witness." Cf. *Social Witness and Evangelism* (The Epworth Press, Publishers, 1943).

Chapter II. The Church in Perspective

1. The New Testament understands by *oikoumenē,* "the community of the *gentiles,* mankind who with their religion, culture, and politics is doomed to perdition," and *never* the Christian *oikoumenē.* Thus, correctly, M. Paeslack, "Die Oikumene im N.T.," *Theologia Viatorum,* 1950, pp. 33–47. However, it is unwarranted when Paeslack separates this meaning from the idea of the "mission field." Too easily he smuggles away Matt. 24:14 (p. 46).

2. R. Liechtenhan, *Die urchristliche Mission* (Zürich, 1946), p. 32. For this whole chapter, see the studies of O. Cullmann, "Le caractère eschatologique du devoir mission- aire," *R.H.Ph.R.,* 1936, pp. 210–245; "Eschatologie und Mis- sion im N.T.," *E.M.M.,* 1941, pp. 98–108, and his summary in *Christus und die Zeit* (Zürich, 1946), pp. 138–153.

3. Th. Preiss, "L'Église et la mission," in *La Lumière des Nations* (Neuchâtel, 1944), p. 20; M. Leenhardt, "Mission Structure de l'église," in M. Goguel, ed., *Le Problème de l'église* (Paris, 1947), pp. 123 ff.

4. Cf. W. Lütgert, "Mission und Geschichtsphilosophie," in *Reich Gottes und Weltgeschichte* (Gütersloh, 1928), pp. 1–12; E. Seeberg, *Menschwerdung und Geschichte* (Stuttgart, 1938), pp. 41 f.

5. O. Michel, "Menschensohn und Völkerwelt," *E.M.Z.,* 1941, pp. 257–267; cf. also K. Barth, *Auslegung von Mat. 28:16–10* (Basel, 1945).

6. Important in this connection is the study of G. Bertram, "Das Antike Judentum als Missionsreligion," in G. Rosen, *Juden und Phönizier* (Tübingen, 1929), pp. 22–68.

7. Bertram, *op. cit.,* p. 30.

8. V. Herntrich, *Theologische Wörterbuch zum Neuen Testament,* III, article on "Krino," pp. 932 ff. E. Sellin, "Die Lösung des deuterojesanischen Gottesknechtsrätsel," *Z.A.W.,* 1937, p. 188 of "Gottesordnung," Isa. 40:14, 51:4, 52:7.

9. Sellin, *loc. cit.*, p. 190.

10. G. Bertram, *loc. cit.*, pp. 35 f.

11. O. Michel, "Gottesherrschaft und Völkerwelt," *E.M.Z.*, 1941, pp. 225–232; cf. Strack-Billerbeck, III (1926), p. 310.

12. E. Stauffer, *Theologie des N. T.* (Geneva, 1945), p. 203; Cf. O. Michel, "Gottesherrschaft," *loc cit.*, *passim*.

13. B. Sundkler, *Jésus et les païens* (Uppsala, 1937). For a criticism, see Liechtenhan, *op. cit.*, p. 37. See especially H. Schlier, "Die Entscheidung für die Heidenmission in der Urchristenheit," *E.M.Z.*, 1942, pp. 166–183, 208–215.

14. Sundkler, *op. cit.*, pp. 35, 65.

15. Among those who agree are R. Bultmann, *O.L.Z.*, 1939, pp. 302 f.; N.A. Dahl, *Das Volk Gottes* (Oslo, 1941), p. 145; and now especially A. G. Hebert, *The Throne of David*, pp. 33 ff., 211 ff.

16. H. Schlier, *loc. cit.*, pp. 172–174.

17. K. Barth, *Kirchliche Dogmatik*, II, 2, pp. 327 ff.; K. L. Schmidt, *Die Judenfrage im Lichte von Römer 9–11* (Zürich, 1943), pp. 37 ff.

18. H. Schlier, *loc. cit.*, p. 177.

19. F. Büchsel, *Der Geist Gottes im N. T.* (1926), p. 357; H. D. Wendland, *Schriftgebundenheit und Geistesleitung in der urchristlichen Mission.*

20. W. Michaelis, "Geist Gottes und Mission nach dem N.T.," *E.M.M.*, 1932, pp. 5–16. O. Cullmann, *E.M.M.*, 1941, p. 101.

21. For this section, cf. K. H. Rengstorf, "Apostolos," *Theologische Wörterbuch zum Neuen Testament*, I, pp. 397–448; G. Sasz, *Der paulinische Apostelbegriff* (Greifswald, 1938).

22. Rengstorf, *loc. cit.*, p. 435; E. Peterson, "To be an apostle means especially: to be sent from the Jews to the Gentiles," *Die Kirche aus den Juden und Heiden* (Würzberg, 1933), p. 16.

23. For this "prophetic concept of apostleship," cf. G. Sasz, *op. cit.*, pp. 41 ff.

24. Cf. Sasz, *op. cit.*, pp. 30, 39. The division at the council of Jerusalem is meant geographically (*eis ethne*, "in the territory of the diaspora"), not ethnographically; cf. R. Liechtenhan, *op. cit.*, p. 78.

25. A. Fridrichsen, *The Apostle and His Message* (Uppsala, 1947), p. 4.

26. H. Schlier, *op. cit.,* pp. 178 f.

27. Liechtenhan, *op. cit.,* pp. 66, 72; cf. G. Sasz, *op. cit.* p. 71.

28. G. Sasz, *op. cit.* p. 48.

29. H. W. Gensichen, "Grundfragen der Kirchwerdung in der Mission," *Evangelische Missions Zeitschrift,* 1951, pp. 33–46.

30. J. L. Leuba, *L'Institution et l'evénement* (Neuchâtel, 1950).

31. M. Paeslack; "Die Oikumene im N.T.," in *Theologia Viatorum,* 1950, pp. 33–47. Cf. G. Bornkamm, "Christus und die Welt in der urchristlichen Botschaft," in *Zeitschrift für Theologie und Kirche,* 1950, pp. 212–226.

32. H. D. Wendland, *Die Eschatologie des Reiches Gottes bei Jesus* (1931), p. 246. Cf. also E. Käseman, "Phil. 2:5–11," in *Zeitschrift für Theologie und Kirche,* 1950, pp. 313–360.

33. Cf., on the inner dynamics of the Word of God and its significance for the proclamation, the important study by G. Wingren, *Predikan* (Lund, 1949).

34. More recent researches on the apostolate of the early Christians entail a correction of the traditional conception of the apostle (e.g., the idea of an apostolic *numerus clausus,* eyewitness-ship) as a necessary requirement of the apostolic ministry (secondary only), etc., and emphasize that the gospel and the apostolate are "conceptions which are connected with each other" and that "the [Pauline] apostolate receives its essential meaning from the missionary idea." Cf., e.g., H. von Campenhausen, "Der urchristliche Apostelbegriff" in *Studia Theologica,* I, 1, 1947, pp. 96–131; H. Mosbeck, "Apostolos in the N.T.," *loc. cit.,* II, 2, 1950, pp. 166–200; and J. Munck, "Paul, the Apostles and the Twelve," *loc. cit.,* III, 1, 1950, pp. 96–110.

It is not only a peculiarity of contemporary Dutch theology (as is so often assumed) that one tries to understand the church by taking the apostolate ("mission") as its essence. One finds the same thought, to mention only one example, in T. W. Manson, *The Church's Ministry* (The Westminster

Press, 1949), e.g., p. 32: "It is a pity . . . that the word "apostolic" has had its meaning narrowed in the course of centuries, so that instead of declaiming primarily the church's commitment to a great missionary task it merely registers a claim on the part of the Eastern and Roman Communions to be lawful successors of the apostles"; p. 34: "The church is 'apostolic' in virtue of doing the work of an Apostle," etc.

35. Cf. K. Barth, *Kirchliche Dogmatik*, III, 4 (1951), pp. 538 ff.

36. W. Elert, *Das christliche Ethos* (1949), p. 555.

37. J. Bonsirven, *Théologie du Nouveau Testament* (1951), pp. 155 ff.

38. L. S. Thornton, *The Common Life in the Body of Christ* (London: The Dacre Press, 1942).

39. The contrast proselytizing mission has been worked out with special sharpness by S. Aalen, *Licht und Finsternis im A.T.* . . . (Oslo, 1951), pp. 88 ff., 202 ff., 282 ff.

Chapter III. Apostolate: Communicating with Fellow Travelers

1. For this characterization, see Alfred Weber, *Kulturgeschichte als Kultursoziologie* (1950), especially pp. 416 ff.: "Kommt der vierte Mensch?" An interesting discussion of Weber's concept can be found in the symposium *Kommt der vierte Mensch?* (Ropke, *et al.*), 1952.

2. C. Moeller, "Le sens de Dieu dans la littérature contemporaine," in *Lumen Vitae*, 1952, pp. 367–384.

3. A. D. Muller, *Prometheus oder Christus?* (1948).

4. This is clearly shown in an analysis of the post-Christian situation (in a section of Brussels); see *La Mèche qui fume encore* (1949), by J. de Vincennes and Cl. Olivier.

5. This attitude with respect to the minister is movingly portrayed in H. Hatzfeld's novel *La Flamme et le Vent* (1952) the Reformed counterpart of Barnanos' *Journal d'un Curé de Campagne*.

6. J. A. T. Robinson, "The Theological College in a Changing World," in *Theology*, 1952, pp. 202–208.

7. For the whole complex of questions concerning communication, see R. Jolivet, *Essai sur les Problèmes et les Conditions de la Sincérité* (1950).

8. Cf. H. Thielicke, *Theologie der Anfechtung* (1949), pp. 265 ff.

9. Thus still frequently in Anglo-Saxon evangelistic literature: Elmer Homrighausen, *Choose Ye This Day* (The Westminster Press, 1943). Bryan Green, *The Practice of Evangelism* (Charles Scribner's Sons, 1951).

10. L. Rétif, *Catéchisme et Mission Ouvrière* (1950). Bishop Hans Lilje especially has repeatedly pointed to dialogue as a modern form of witness, most recently in "Wege der Verkündigung," in *Theologie und Liturgie*, 1952, pp. 341 ff.

11. This is magnificently demonstrated in J. Monnerot's works *Sociologie du Communisme* (1949), and *Déplacements du Sacré*, pp. 428 ff.

12. K. F. Helleiner gives the following explanation for what is called the "temporary block-out of religious faculties": The best religious elements were wiped out in history during religious wars and persecutions of heretics, or they disappeared in the monastery without leaving a religious heritage. ("A Change in Religious Aptitude?" in *Review of Religion*, 1952, pp. 151 ff.)

13. For instance, what T. R. Morton writes about "The Emerging Pattern of Churchlife" in his important booklet *The Household of Faith* (1951), pp. 98 ff. (American ed., *The Community of Faith*, Association Press, 1954).

14. Cf. Péguy in *Jeanne d'Arc:* "The faith which I love says the Lord, is hope . . . hope, says the Lord, that's what amazes me. Even me! That's what is amazing. That the poor children see what takes place and that they believe that tomorrow it will be better. . . . "

Chapter V. The Life of the Christian Community

1. By "categorial churches" those churches generally are meant which—in distinction from the parish (= territorially determined congregation)—are oriented toward groups in

198 THE CHURCH INSIDE OUT

society that do not have to live together in a "cadastrally defined area."

2. Thus, for instance, the students figure in the chapter on
the mission situation in A. J. Bronkhorst's *Schrift en Kerk-
orde* (The Hague, 1947), p. 273.

3. H. Obendiek, "Die Kirche in der Missionssituation,"
Evangelische Theologie, 1950/1, p. 108.

4. G. W. O. Addleshaw, *The Beginnings of the Parochial
System* (London, 1953). B. van Leeuwen in *Levende Zielzorg*
(Utrecht, 1954), pp. 107 ff. In the Eastern churches the
forming of parishes developed somewhat differently.

5. J. Brouwers, *Nieuwe Wegen in de Zielzorg* (Bilthoven,
1956), pp. 20 ff.

6. E.g., in the study project "The Structure of a Missionary
Church."

7. Cf. the report from the Oberlin Conference (1957)
entitled *The Impact of Mobility as It Affects the Work of the
Churches in the U.S.A.* This report, which can be found in
The Nature of the Unity We Seek, ed. by Paul S. Minear
(Bethany Press, 1958), pp. 275–288, is very important for the
European situation as well.

8. E. R. Wickham, *Church and People in an Industrial City*
(London: The Lutterworth Press, 1957), p. 251.

9. T. W. Manson, *The Church's Ministry* (The Westminster
Press, 1948), p. 18.

10. H. von Campenhausen, *Kirchliches Amt und geistliche
Vollmacht in der ersten drei Jahrhunderten* (Tübingen, 1953),
pp. 70 f. Compare with this the following statement by
E. Schweitzer: "Presbyters are never mentioned by Paul. In
Phil. 1:1 he mentions bishops and deacons, both occurring in
the plural in a single church. Other letters, however, in particular I Corinthians, prove that there was no authoritative
office at all. In Corinth Paul knew no one to whose authority
he could appeal for the proper administration of the Lord's
Supper. He could only appeal to the entire Christian community to purge the celebration of foreign elements." "Unity
and Diversity in the N.T. Teaching Regarding the Church,"
Theology Today, 1957, p. 480.

11. J. Knox, "The Ministry in the Primitive Church," in
The Ministry in Historical Perspectives, ed. by H. Richard

Niebuhr and Daniel D. Williams (Harper & Row, Publishers, Inc., 1956), p. 2.

12. Schweitzer, *loc. cit.*, pp. 480 f.

13. Von Campenhausen, *op. cit.*, p. 74. In other parts of the New Testament the accents are put a little differently, but the basic theme remains the same. Compare for this whole section M. Barth, *The Broken Wall* (The Judson Press, 1959), where, on the basis of the book of Ephesians, the mission church in which the offices function is pictured.

14. G. Bornkamm, "Herrenmahl und Kirche bei Paulus," *Zeitschrift für Theologie und Kirche*, 1946, p. 333.

15. E. Schlink, "Lord's Supper or Church's Supper," *Student World*, 1950, p. 53.

16. A. C. Outler, *The Christian Tradition and the Unity We Seek* (Oxford University Press, 1957), p. 77.

17. Cf. T. Torrance: "Unity can never be reached so long as the separate Churches refuse to give each other the divine medicine for their healing," *Intercommunion* (London, 1952), p. 349.

18. C. W. Mönnich, G. C. Van Niftrik, *Hervormd-Luthers Gesprek over het Avondmaal* (Nijkerk, 1958), p. 193.

19. Here I follow G. Bornkamm's interpretation of I Cor., ch. 11, *loc. cit.*, pp. 312–349.

20. W. Jannasch, "Abendmahl," in *R.G.G.*, I³, pp. 47 f.

21. In an (anonymous) article on "Intercommunion" the suggestion is made that the restoration of the Table fellowship can serve as "not a solution, but an easing of our tensions," *Ecumenical Review*, 1949, p. 444. Cf. G. I. F. Thomson, "The Revival of the Agape," in *Intercommunion*, pp. 388–396.

22. J. Sittler, cited in *The Nature of the Unity We Seek*, p. 204.

23. In I Cor. 11:20 the fellowship meal and the subsequent Communion together are called "the Lord's Supper."

24. From the memorandum *The Calling of the Church to Mission and Unity*, 1951.

25. K. Barth, *Kirchliche Dogmatik*, IV/3, 1 (1959), pp. 38 ff.

26. L. Newbigin, *One Body, One Gospel, One World* (International Missionary Council, 1961), p. 54.

Chapter VII. Church and Race

1. F. Loescher, *Protestant Churches and the Negro* (Association Press, 1948), pp. 16, 106.

2. See the studies of Dr. Hans Schärer concerning the Ngadju-Dyaks.

3. For this paragraph, see O. Michel, "Gottesherrschaft und Völkerwelt," *E. M. Z.*, 1941; J. Blauw, *Goden en Mensen* (1950).

4. For this paragraph, see J. Lüthner, *Hellenen und Barbaren* (1923). Also J. Kaerst, *Die Antike Idee der Oekumene* (1903), p. 18: "Also that which is originally not-Greek, is now, by conceiving of it as universally human, inwardly adjusted to the Greek world. Under the concept of the rational it is incorporated in the sphere of the ideally Greek."

5. This can be studied most clearly in the development of classes among the modern bourgeoisie. Cf. E. Goblot, *La Barrière et Le Niveau* (1925).

6. In American sociology the viewing of the race question as a caste question is rather general: K. G. Myrdal, *The American Dilemma* (Harper & Row, Publishers, Inc., 1944); F. W. Wertheim, *Het Rassenprobleem, ondergang van een mythe* (1950).

7. *The Race Question*, Statement issued by UNESCO, July 18, 1950.

8. C. F. Höffner, *Christentum und Menschenwürde, Das Anliegen der spanischen Kolonialethik im goldenen Zeitalter* (1947). Lewis Hanke, *The Spanish Struggle for Justice in the Conquest of America*, (University of Pennsylvania Press, 1949).

9. See the report of the congress that was exclusively concerned with the Bantu problem, entitled *Die Naturellenvraagstuk* (1950).

10. P. van Biljon, *Grensbakens tussen Blank en Swart in Suid Afrika* (1947). Cf. Report of Rosettenville-Conference, 1949, *The Christian Citizen in a Multiracial Society*, p. 49.

11. E. Roux, *Time Longer Than Rope* (1949), p. 33.

12. Cited in *Kulturgeskiedenis van die Afrikaner* (1945), p. 339.

13. B. G. M. Sundkler, *Bantu Prophets in South Africa,* (Oxford University Press, 1948).

Chapter IX. Safety Last

1. Cf. J. Filson, ed., *On the Move to Unity* (1962).

2. A full discussion in G. Niemeier, ed., *Lehrgespräch über das heilige Abendmahl* (1961).

3. T. F. Torrance in *Intercommunion* (1952), p. 349.

4. Report of the General Synod of the Reformed Church in the Netherlands: *Open and Ecumenical Communion* (1962).

5. A. B. Come, *Agents of Reconciliation* (The Westminster Press, 1960), p. 43.

6. S. Grundmann, *Der lutherische Weltbund* (1957), pp. 408 ff.

7. Many similar examples in: *Intercommunion* (1952); *Koinonia* (1957); Th. Sartory, *Die Eucharistie im Verständnis der Konfessionen* (1961).

8. D. T. Niles, *Upon the Earth* (McGraw-Hill Book Company, Inc., 1962), p. 145.

9. Lambeth Conference, 1930, on "economy."

10. H. Dombois, *Das Recht der Gnade: Oekumenisches Kirchenrecht,* I (1961), pp. 171 f., 843 ff.

11. Cf. also the Anglican-Orthodox Interburial Consensus of 1869/1870.

12. The crucial words in II Cor. 5:17, *kaine ktisis,* can be translated like this. Compare the footnote in the New English Bible for this text.

13. Cf. also H. Dombois, *loc. cit.,* p. 264.

14. F. A. Cockin, *God in Action: A Study of the Holy Spirit* (Penguin Books, Inc., 1961), p. 183.

Chapter X. On the Way to the World of Tomorrow

1. Chad Walsh, *Early Christians of the 21st Century* (Harper & Row, Publishers, Inc., 1950).

2. L. P. Hartley, *Facial Justice* (Doubleday & Company, Inc., 1961).

3. M. L. Ernst, *Utopia 1976* (Rinehart & Company, Inc., 1955).

4. Romano Guardini, *Das Ende der Neuzeit* (Basel, 1950). (The title of the Dutch translation of this book is *De gestalte der toekonst* (*The Shape of the Future*).

5. Among others, K. Brockmüller, *Das Christentum am Morgen des Atomzeitalters* (Frankfurt, 1955); H. Vogel, *Um die Zukunft des Menschen im atomaren Zeitalter* (Berlin, 1960).

6. E. Fromm, *Der moderne Mensch und seine Zukunft* (*The Sane Society*) (Frankfurt, 1960).

7. P. F. Drucker, *Kengetal vor Morgan* (*The Landmarks of Tomorrow*) (Bussum, 1959), p. 10.

8. J. G. Bomhoff, "Literatuur als spiegel van onze tijd," in *De Maatschappij van nu en morgen* (Amsterdam, 1958), p. 120; cf. also *Wending*, 1960/1, p. 482.

9. G. Anders, *Die Antiquiertheit des Menschen* (Munich, 1956).

10. "Lobet die Kalte, die Finsternis und das Verderben,/ Schauet hinan!/ Es kommt nicht auf euch an,/ Und ihr könnt unbesorgt sterben." In *Grosser Dankchoral*.

11. J. Fourastié, *Le grand espoir du XXᵉ siècle* (Paris, 1958), p. 236.

12. What this experimental living means for the Christian has been very well described by H. Schmidt in *Vita experimentalis* (Munich, 1959).

13. Fourastié, *op. cit.*, pp. 217 f.; cf. B. Pohl, "Freizeit in Utopia," in *Monatsschrift für Pastoraltheologie* (1960), pp. 139 ff.

14. H. H. Schrey in *Verantwortung für den Menschen* (Festschrift Held) (Stuttgart, 1957), pp. 209 ff.

15. Among others, E. R. Wickham, *Church and People in an Industrial City,* London, 1957; H. Storck, *Kirche im Neuland der Industrie* (Berlin, 1959); J. Schasching, *Kirche und industrielle Gesellschaft* (Vienna, 1960).

16. Ernst, *op. cit.*, p. 194, suggests this.

17. Guardini, *op. cit.*, pp. 85 f.

18. Schmidt, *op. cit.*, p. 82.

19. H. J. Margull, *Theologie der missionarischen Verkündigung* (Stuttgart, 1959), pp. 172 ff.; cf. Wickham, *op. cit.*, pp. 177 ff.

20. H. O. Wölber, *Religion ohne Entscheidung: Volkskirche*

am Beispiel der jungen Generation (Göttingen, 1959). Cf. V. Herntrich: "The fellowship in the *Volkskirche* is surrounded by the marks of 'commonness' and 'indecision.' He who without a conscious decision has become a member of the *Volkskirche*, will not easily come to a decision when he is once in it." In *Die evangelische Kirche in Deutschland* (Stuttgart, 1959), pp. 150 f. (In order to prevent misunderstanding, Herntrich holds that one may not give up the *Volkskirche*.)

21. H. D. Wendland, *Die Kirche in der modernen Gesellschaft* (Hamburg, 1956), pp. 45 ff.

22. N. Goodall, "The New Frontiers of the Church's World Mission," in *The Ecumenical Era in Church and Society,* New York, 1959, pp. 109 f.; cf. R. M. Fagley, *Population Explosion and Christian Responsibility* (Oxford University Press, 1960).

23. Wickham, *op. cit.,* pp. 170 ff.

24. A. Toynbee, "The Diaspora Age," in *Issues,* September, 1960. "In the new age, on which we are now entering, the standard type of community . . . is going to be the world encompassing religious community. It is, in fact, going to be the type of community that has been represented already, for some 2400 years past, by the Jewish Diaspora."

25. "Our Call to Be a Minority," in *Laity,* No. 8, 1959 (Geneva).

26. W. and H. P. M. Goddijn, *Godsdienstsociologie* (Utrecht, 1960), pp. 96 f.

27. H. Berkhof, "De oecumenische kaart van Nederland," in *Oecumene in het Vizier* (Amsterdam, 1960), pp. 34 f.

BIBLIOGRAPHY

A Books and brochures
B Contributions to books, symposiums, lexicons
C Articles in periodicals and journals
D Published addresses
E Publications of the World Council of Churches
F Publications of various organizations
G Available in offset
H Available in mimeographed form (limited supply)

1941 1. A *Vragen der Wereldkerk,* Guidebook for mission-study circles (Zeist).

1944 2. DFH *Introduction presentée lors des entretiens de Présinge* (WCSF, Geneva) (cf. number 7).

3. B "Dit swaer tempeest" and "En Indië . . . ?" in *Luctor et Emergo* (presented to the Netherlanders in Switzerland at the occasion of August 31, 1944), pp. 28–33 and 57–61, respectively.

4. C "Que doit être une université?" *Alma Mater* (revue universitaire de la Swisse Romande), October, pp. 50–54.

5. C "Dutch Students in Search of the University," *The Student World* 37, pp. 354–355.

1945 6. A *De Wereldzending in oorlogstijd* (Reeks De Strijdende Kerk No. 2) (The Hague).

7. C "The SCM Within the Church and for the Church," *The Student World* 38, pp. 12–21.

8. C "Consolation in Despair," *The Student World* 38, pp. 281–285.

1946 9. B Introduction and Notes for *Zending in Indonesië*, Report of the missionary conference in Batavia, 1946 (The Hague).

1947 10. CD "La Mission et le nationalisme," *Le Monde non-chrétien*, pp. 390 ff.

1948 11. A *Kerk en volk in de Duitse zendingswetenschap*, dissertation (Amsterdam).

12. C "Our Task in the Growing Church," *The Student World* 41, pp. 369–374.

1949 13. AC *Deelgenoten in verantwoordelijkheid*, Afterthoughts concerning the mission conference, Woudschoten, 1949 (Amsterdam). Reprint from *De Heerbaan* 2, pp. 197–235.

14. AE *The Evangelisation of Man in Modern Mass Society* (Study department document, Geneva).

15. C "Geen home base meer," *Wending* 4, pp. 164–169.

16. C "Kroniek 1948," *De Heerbaan* 2, pp. 19–25, 48–53, 81–84.

17. C "Profeten en kerken in Zuid-Afrika," *De Heerbaan* 2, pp. 127–136.

18. C "Losse notities over godsdienstvrijheid," *De Heerbaan* 2, pp. 237–253.

19. C "In gesprek," *De Heerbaan* 2, pp. 343–348.

20. CD "Mission in der Krise," *Evangelische Missions Zeitschrift* 6, III, pp. 1–7.

21. CD "Junge Kirche als dienende Kirche," *Evangelische Missions Zeitschrift* 6, IV, pp. 1–6.

22. C "Gecamoufleerde Toonbank" (review of Dr. H. van Mook, *Indonesië, Nederland en de wereld*), *Wending* 4, p. 219.

23. C "Europe, A Mission Field" ("Reviews"), *The Ecumenical Review* 2, pp. 206–208.

1950 24. C "The Evangelisation of Man in Modern Mass Society," *The Ecumenical Review* 3, pp. 133–140 (cf. number 14).

25. C   "The Call to Evangelism," *International Review of Missions* 39, pp. 162–175.

26. C   "Orde, milieu, mens," *Wending* 5, pp. 284–297.

27. C   "Nieuwe leren zakken," *De Heerbaan* 3, pp. 309–322.

28. C   "Nineteenth-Century Missionary Impetus" (review of W. Holsten, *Joh. Baptista Goszner: Glaube und Gemeinde*), *International Review of Missions* 39, p. 219.

1951 29. AE   *Evangelism in France*, Ecumenical Studies (Geneva).

30. C   "Jongleurs op Rhodos," *De Heerbaan* 4, pp. 101–108.

31. CD   "Enkele opmerkingen over 'Kerk en Ras' in het bijzonder met het oog op Zuid-Afrika," *De Heerbaan* 4, pp. 253–266.

32. C   "Mission und Oekumene," *Evangelisches Missions Magazin* 95, pp. 146–156 (cf. number 36); French: *Le Monde non-chrétien*, pp. 327–340.

33. C   "Gesprek onder-weg," *In de Waagschaal* 6, pp. 348–350.

34. EH   *New Forms of Evangelism?* Preparatory material for the European layman's conference (Geneva).

35. FH   *The Theology of Evangelism (and Missions)*, A study and discussion outline prepared for theological students (WCSF, Geneva).

1952 36. CF   "Mission und Oekumene," in *Die Botschaft von Jesus Christus in einer nicht-christlichen Welt*, published by Studentenbund für Mission, pp. 18–24 (number 32).

37. C   "Die Kirche im Missionsdenken," *Evangelische Missions Zeitschrift* 9, I, pp. 1–13.— English: "The Church in Missionary Thinking," *International Review of Missions* 41, pp. 324–336.—French: "L'Église dans la

pensée missionaire," *Le Monde non-chré-tion*, pp. 415–433.—Danish: *Nordisk Missiens Tidsskrift, maart.*

38. C   "The Varieties of Evangelistic Experience" ("Reviews"), *The Ecumenical Review* 4, pp. 208–211.

39. C   "Evangelism—The Raison d'être of the Church" ("Reviews"), *The Ecumenical Review* 4, pp. 431–435.

40. C   "Rondom het apostolaat," *Wending* 7, pp. 547–554 (cf. numbers 41 and 77).

1953 41. C   "Missionsepigonen" and "Apostolat und Vierter Mensch," *Die Zeichen der Zeit*, Nos. 7 and 8 (number 40).

42. C   "Die Theologie des 'vierten' Menschen," *Die Neue Furche* 7, pp. 391–397 (number 41, abridged).

43. C   "Ende und Anfang der Verkündigung," *Quatember* (evangelische Jahresbriefe), 17, 2, pp. 70–76 (see also number 58).

44. A   *Kirche in Frankreich auf neuen Wegen* (Berlin) (number 29).

45. CD   "Het apostolaat in Europa in het licht van enkele ervaringen van de Islam-zending," *Nederlands Theologisch Tijdschrift* 7, pp. 321–331.

46. AD   *Getemperd Ongeduld*, Inaugural address at the University of Utrecht (Nijkerk).

47. C   "Priester-arbeiders in Frankrijk," *Woord en Dienst* 2, pp. 349–350.

48. C   "Monsieur Montuclard," *Woord en Dienst* 2, pp. 382–383.

49. CD   "Tranen over Johannesburg," *Hervormd Utrecht* 8, pp. 680–681.

50. B   Preface to N. G. J. van Schouwenburg, *De Kerk maar sluiten . . . ?* (Baarn).

51. CDFH   "Heel de kerk voor heel de wereld." Lecture delivered at the Conference of the Ecumenical Youth Council, *Oecumenisch Jeugdnieuws* IV, 2, pp. 2–10.

52. BDFH *Het apostolaat onder de buitenkerkelijken,* Lecture delivered at the Conference of Chaplains in Labor Camps.

53. DFH *Address Before the I.K.O.R. Conference* (published by I. K. O. R.).

1954 54. CF "Mission—Heute!" in *Mission—Heute!* published by Studentenbund für Mission, pp. 5–12.

55. C "Aanloop naar de evangelistiek," *Woord en Dienst* 3, pp. 194–195, 214–215, 230, 242, 250–251, 258–259.

1955 56. C "De gestalte van de kerk," *Woord en Dienst* 4, pp. 163–164, 179–180.

1956 57. C "Uitgesteld Jubeljaar," *Wending* 11, pp. 201–209.

58. C "Ende und Anfang der Verkündigung," *Das missionarische Wort* 9, pp. 261–266 (number 43).

59. C "Pantomime van het heil," *Wending* 11, pp. 680–693.

60. B "Faculteit der Godgeleerdheid, Prae-advies," *Universiteit en Hogeschool* 2 (1956), pp. 198–210.

1959 61. CF "Buurmans Gek," in *Studentenhuisgemeente,* Elthetobrochurereeks No. 3, pp. 15–28.

62. C "Zending in de stad," *Hervormd Utrecht* 14 (Special Issue, May 1, "Land in Zicht"), pp. 2–4, 6–8.

63. C "Om te beginnen, vragen naar aanleiding van de Hervormde Kerkbouwactie," *Wending* 14, pp. 565–569.

1960 64. B "Over het proselitisme," in *Oecumene in 't vizier, feestbundel* in honor of Dr. W. A. Visser 't Hooft (Amsterdam), pp. 101–110 (cf. number 84).

65. B "Evangelisation," in *Weltkirchenlexicon* (Stuttgart), pp. 378–384.

66. C " 'Ontwakend Afrika' en de zending," *Wending* 15, pp. 281–301.

67. C   "Aanloop naar de evangelistiek," *Woord en Dienst* 9, pp. 100–101 (continuing number 55).

68. DFG   *Naar één evangelische kerk in Nederland?* Three radio speeches (published by I. K. O. R.).

69. CDFG   *Spoorzoeken in onze tijd,* Woord en Daad Series, No. 3 (Centraal Bond voor Inwendige Zending en christelijk maatschappelijk werk, Amsterdam).

70. CDEG   *The Renewal: Mission and Unity of the Local Church,* Lecture at the Ecumenical Youth Assembly in Europe, Lausanne, *Youth* 2, October, pp. 64–67.

71. CDFG   *Op weg naar de wereld van morgen, Horstcahier "Kerk en Wereld"* No. 9 (Driebergen), pp. 45–70 (cf. numbers 76 and 85).

1961 72. B   "Säkularismus; II in Asien und Afrika," in *Die Religion in Geschichte und Gegenwart* (3), V (Tübingen), pp. 1296–1299.

73. C   "Boekbespreking" (K. S. Latourette, *Christianity in a Revolutionary Age* I and II), *Tijdschrift voor Geschiedenis* 74, pp. 569–571.

74. CD   "Christ and the World in Modern Age," *The Student World* 54, pp. 75–82.

75. CFH   "Lekenapostolaat," in the study guide *Zout en Licht,* published by the Nederlandse Studenten Zendingscommissie, Amsterdam.

C   —— *Uitzicht* 7, pp. 109–122.

76. CEG   "On the Way to the World of Tomorrow," *Laity* 11, pp. 5–19 (number 71; cf. number 85).

77. B   Reprinting of "Rondom het apostolaat" (number 40), in *Naar de wereld van morgen,* selections from *Wending*—II,Carillonreeks No. 14 (Amsterdam), pp. 16–39.

78. CDFG   *Address for the Landelijk Congress "Jeugd en Evangelie,"* Krab Series, No. 5, pp. 23–36.

79. DFH   *Oekumenische Perspektieven,* Address for the Conference of the Ecumenical Youth Council.

80. DH   *Tradition und Erneuerung der Kirche—ein Gegensatz?* Lecture for the Evangelische theologen-conferentie, Wenen.

1962 81. C   "Na New Delhi," *Wending* 17, pp. 65–68.

82. C   "Coëxistentie met de minste der mijnen," *Ruimte* (issue on coexistence), pp. 31–38.

83. CDFH   *Interne weerstanden tegen het oecumenisch handelen, Information Bulletin of the Ecumenical Youth Conference* I, 4, pp. 4–10.

84. C   "À propos du prosélytisme," *La Revue de L'Evangelisation,* No. 103 (number 64).

85. C   "Restructuration de l' Église," *Revue pour théologie et philosophie* (numbers 71, 76).

86. CEG   "Exceptions, Eschatology and Our Common Practices," in *Many Churches One Table One Church, Youth* 6, December, pp. 63–77.

87. BDF   "Dietrich Bonhoeffer—en verder," Annuarium Collegium Studiosorum Veritas (cf. number 88).

1963 88. CD   "Dietrich Bonhoeffer—en verder," *Ter Elfder Ure* 10, No. 1, pp. 1–11.

89. C   "Honest to God," *Wending* 18, pp. 209–215.

90. CD   "Een veranderende Kerk in een veranderende wereld," *De Strijdende Kerk,* August 31.

91. HE   "The Meaning of Mission (-ary)," *Concept* (Department of Studies on Evangelism, WCC), Special Issue, September 5, pp. 11–19.

92. CD   "De missionaire struktuur van de Gemeente," *Gereformeerd Theologisch Tijdschrift,* pp. 225–238.

93. C   "Kleine Robinsonnade 1963," *Wending* 18, pp. 681–691.

1964 94. B   *Kirche,* Theologie für Nichttheologen II
                (Stuttgart).
      95. C   "Veranderende Kerk in veranderende
                samenleving,"*De Kerkvoogdij,* a monthly
                of the Association of Church Wardens in
                the Netherlands Reformed Church, July-
                August, pp. 1244 ff.